Nelson Thornes **Framework English**

Skills in Fiction

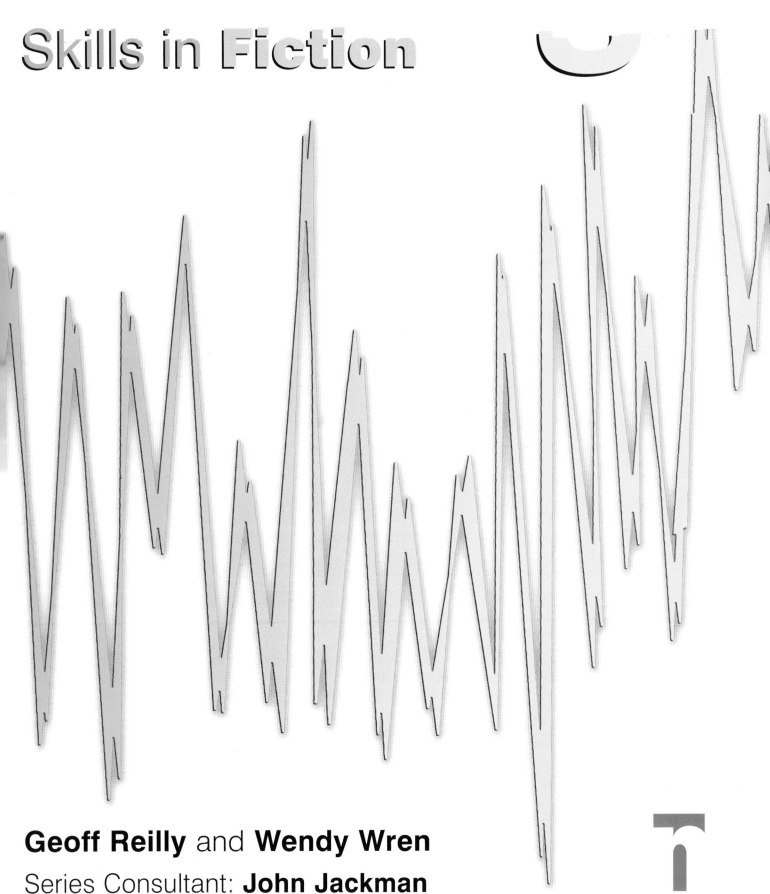

Geoff Reilly and **Wendy Wren**

Series Consultant: **John Jackman**

Contents

Maximus Meridas

In the film, Gladiator, *Maximus Meridas, General of the Felix Army, has been forced to fight in the arena, as the gladiator known as 'The Spaniard'. In ancient Rome, the Emperor had the absolute power of life and death over those slaves who fought in the arena as gladiators. In this extract from the second draft of the screenplay, Maximus confronts the Emperor.*

Maximus spurs his horse and gallops toward the final chariot –
the charioteer whips his horses and zooms toward Maximus –

The crowd is breathless – watching the final battle –

Maximus and the chariot speed toward each other –
like Medieval jousters – And collide in a flashing explosion of steel –

Maximus sails from his horse – as the charioteer sails from his chariot –
Maximus lands hard but quickly pulls himself up, he races to the final charioteer.
The charioteer is defeated but not dead.

Maximus glances around, all his opponents are defeated.

He stands over the final charioteer. Then he simply tosses down his sword.

The crowd is stunned by this strange act of mercy. But then an enormous roar
grows from the crowd – wave after wave of adulation for the hero of the day.

Maximus looks around, taking it all in. Then he turns to the Imperial Box.
Maximus slowly walks to the Imperial Box. The Praetorian Archers immediately
raise their bows, pointing down at him.

Maximus glares up at Commodus through his helmet mask. Commodus returns
his gaze, curious. The crowd is intrigued, growing quiet. What is going on?

Then Maximus simply turns and begins walking away.

>COMMODUS
>Slave! Who are you?

The Colosseum is suddenly silent. The Emperor is speaking to a gladiator.

Maximus keeps walking.

>COMMODUS
>SLAVE! WHO ARE YOU?

Maximus keeps walking, his fists clenched now.

Commodus suddenly grabs a spear from a nearby Praetorian and hurls it
with perfect aim – the crowd gasps – the spear sails past Maximus –
actually nicking his shoulder – it slices into the sand ahead of Maximus.

Maximus stops.

>COMMODUS
>SLAVE! WHO ARE YOU?!

Maximus can hold it no longer. He spins to Commodus –
ripping off his helmet mask – and THUNDERING:

>MAXIMUS
>I AM MAXIMUS MERIDAS, GENERAL OF THE FELIX REGIMENT OF THE
>ROMAN ARMY AND SERVANT TO THE EMPEROR MARCUS AURELIUS!

Commodus' eyes shoot wide – Lucilla bolts up – Gracchus leans forward – Proximo is stunned – the crowd is mystified –

MAXIMUS

I AM FATHER TO A MURDERED SON AND HUSBAND TO A MURDERED WIFE AND LANDLORD TO A MURDERED WORLD – AND I WILL HAVE VENGEANCE!

The Praetorian Archers tense their bows – ready to kill the defiant slave –

But something extraordinary stops them. Almost as one being the crowd roars – they leap to their feet and thrust their thumbs up! They cheer and stomp their approval of Maximus.

Commodus looks around at the people of Rome, amazed.

He finally plasters on a benevolent smile and thrusts his thumb up! The Praetorians lower their bows.

And the crowd cheers. Never in the long, long history of the Colosseum have they ever seen such a thing.

Maximus leads his gladiators out of the arena.

TEXT LEVEL WORK

Comprehension

A 1 What is a '*gladiator*'?

2 What is an '*arena*'?

3 What are '*jousters*'?

4 What is a '*charioteer*'?

5 What is a '*Praetorian*'?

B 1 Explain what the following words mean:
   a '*adulation*'
   b '*imperial*'
   c '*vengeance*'

2 What impression is created by the use of these phrases:
   a '*zooms towards Maximus*'
   b '*flashing explosion of steel*'
   c '*stunned by this strange act of mercy*'?

3 Why do you think that it is necessary for the writer to say, '*The Emperor is speaking to a gladiator*'?

4 Why do you think that some parts of the screenplay are in capital letters?

C 1 The writer manages to create a growing impression of a relationship between Maximus and Commodus. How does he do this? Find examples to support your opinions.

2 The writer seems to want the audience to respond to the characters in different ways. How would the audience react to the characters of Maximus and Commodus? Give evidence for your opinions.

WORD LEVEL WORK

Vocabulary

Dictionary and contextual work

Use a dictionary and the context of the passage to explain the meaning of the following words:

1 absolute	5 archers	9 nicking
2 benevolent	6 stunned	10 regiment
3 Medieval	7 gaze	11 mystified
4 mercy	8 intrigued	12 Colosseum

Spelling

'gue' endings

Key word: intri**gue**

1 Use the key word in a sentence of your own.

2 Learn these important 'gue' words:

catalo**gue**   lea**gue**   synago**gue**   dialo**gue**

SENTENCE LEVEL WORK

Grammar and punctuation

Present continuous tense

We make the present continuous tense by:

subject + auxiliary verb + main verb
Maximus   is   winning

We use the present continuous tense:

- to describe what is happening now, or for some limited time in the immediate future, eg
  'Maximus keeps walking, his fists clenched now.'
- for events that happen frequently, using the adverb 'always', eg
  'The crowd is always cheering courageous gladiators.'

Some verbs do not follow the rule in the same way, eg
  'I think Commodus fought in the arena.'

The following verbs are exceptions:

- believe, agree, understand, know, remember, forget, mean, doubt, eg
  we don't say *'I am believing you'*, we say *'I believe you'*
- wish, love, hate, like, dislike, imagine, want, eg
  we don't say *'I am loving you'*, we say *'I love you'*
- have, own, belong, want, eg
  we don't say *'I am owning ...'*, we say *'I own ...'*
- cost, seem, appear, need, weigh, prefer, recognise, taste, eg
  we don't say *'It is costing ...'*, we say *'It costs ...'*.

Write out these sentences, underlining the main present continuous verb tenses.

1　Maximus spurs his horse and gallops toward the final chariot.
2　The charioteer whips his horses and zooms toward Maximus.
3　Maximus and the chariot speed toward each other and collide in a flashing explosion of steel.
4　Maximus glances around, all his opponents are defeated.
5　Then he turns and slowly walks to the Imperial Box.
6　Maximus glares up at Commodus through his helmet mask.
7　Then Maximus simply turns and begins walking away.
8　Commodus suddenly grabs a spear from a nearby Praetorian and hurls it with perfect aim.
9　They cheer and stomp their approval of Maximus.
10　Commodus looks around at the people of Rome, amazed.
11　He finally plasters on a benevolent smile and thrusts his thumb up!
12　Maximus leads his gladiators out of the arena.

TEXT LEVEL WORK

Writing

Dialogue

> Screenplays or scripts include sections of conversation between characters: this is called *dialogue*. In *Gladiator*, the writer begins the screenplay with extended stage directions. There is brief dialogue in the second half of the extract.
>
> The writer sets up the plot situation in the first half of the extract – the meeting between Maximus and Commodus.
>
> The two characters interact briefly but confrontationally, giving the reader background information on the situation.
>
> The characters are 'developed' through the dialogue: we learn that Maximus has been bereft of his wife and son; we learn that his country has been usurped by a tyrant. Above all, we learn that Maximus will seek revenge on Commodus.

Language features

Dialogue

- Gives the reader information about a character's personality, occupation, nationality, social position/class. In *Gladiator*, we gain a clear impression of Maximus' personality from his behaviour and speech. We know his occupation as a gladiator and slave but we also know that he is honourable. We are able to guess his nationality and his social position from the information provided.

- Advances the action by referring to the main conflict and shows conversational give and take between characters. In *Gladiator*, apart from the fighting in the arena, the writer communicates the sense of a struggle between Maximus and Commodus.

- Sounds like ordinary speech but is appropriate for the context, eg

  *'I am Maximus Meridas, General of the Felix Regiment of the
  Roman Army and servant to the Emperor Marcus Aurelius!'*

  In this example, Maximus is speaking formally to emphasise his pride in his profession and his social status. It also conveys his courage and asserts his sense of himself.

- Develops a better understanding of the characters, and helps the scene to progress, eg

  The continued repetition of *'Slave! Who are you?'* by Commodus establishes that Maximus is a strong enough character to resist the demands of the Emperor. The repetition develops a better understanding of the characters, illustrating Maximus' willingness to risk offending the Emperor and his control over his own actions.

- Avoids the characters explaining the plot or repeating information for the audience, eg

  *'I am father to a murdered son and husband to a murdered wife
  and landlord to a murdered world – and I will have vengeance!'*

  (Note the repetition of the word 'murdered'.) When he says *'landlord to a murdered world'*, Maximus is stating that the Emperor has been murdering his own citizens and that he, Maximus, is taking on the responsibility of overthrowing Commodus – *'and I will have vengeance!'*

Stage directions

In a play, the writer provides information for the actors and directors on how the scene should be played, eg 'Exit stage right'.

In a film script, the writer may indicate camera shots, movements, angles, special effects and timings beside the dialogue, eg 'low shot', 'pans left to close-up of clock', 'sound of ticking for 3 seconds'.

In the screenplay for *Gladiator*, the writer has broken with the conventional way of providing information. He has provided descriptive prose information instead.

Writing assignment

Imagine that you are Commodus, the Emperor. Using the information in the extract, write both sides of the conversation that Commodus would have, describing to a friend what happened at the Colosseum. Explain how you (Commodus) and Maximus reacted to the events. What would be your plans now?

Use the information in the language features to help you to write the dialogue. Don't forget to include stage directions. Check that you have laid out the dialogue and stage directions correctly.

two upturned kegs

In eighteenth century England, Jess is a young girl, who has been apprenticed to the blacksmith, Samson Orry. She has been virtually a slave, in all but name. Samson sells Jess in a pub but she escapes. On the run, she tries to hide on a ship but is caught. There she meets Midnight, a slave from Africa, who is owned by the captain of the ship.

'What's to become of me?' Jess ventured to ask.

They were sitting on two upturned kegs in the dark of the fo'c'sle – had been sitting forever and longer, she felt. A square of light coming through the open hatch, made half-hearted patterns through the ladder and silhouetted the Negro. He didn't answer and Jess felt uneasy, but having started to talk was determined not to be ignored. Perhaps he hadn't understood her?

'What'll the Cap'n do with me? How long do us have to stay here?'

Midnight shrugged. 'We stay until it is his pleasure that we go.'

Jess was startled, not by the idea, but by the way it was expressed. He sounded almost like the gentlemen who brought their horses to be shod at Samson's smithy, except for a slight foreign way of leaning on the wrong part of the words. It was not the speech of a deckhand. She'd heard enough of them cussing and blinding.

'Thee his servant?' she asked.

'Slave,' he corrected.

She looked at the polished coppery band, so different from the collars Samson forged along with fetters and thumbscrews for the slave trade. They were rough spiked things. 'Never seen a slave band like that afore.' He seemed uninterested, so she tried asking:

'Where do th'come from?'

'Here.'

'I mean afore that?'

'Jamaica.'

'And the Guinea Coast afore that?' she prompted, hoping for tales about unknown Africa that seemed to her as strange as the moon and as far away.

But he wouldn't answer and only shifted, rattling the chain.

'I've seen 'em loading up the Guineamen ready to sail for Africa,' she said, thrusting away the indignity of being shackled, cheering herself with talk. 'They take all sorts of fancy things to trade – brass basins, beads, looking glasses … last time I saw great bales of cotton stuffs, all red and blue and gold. Like sunsets they were … lovely!' She sighed, coveting the memory, then went on: 'Did the Cap'n buy thee from the Guinea Coast and ship thee across the sea?' She was determined to get an answer.

But his reply was a list of questions: 'What of you? Your name, your trade, your place of living?'

She stiffened, suspecting that he was making fun of her. She wasn't going to stand for that! 'Th'tongue's too long,' she said. ''Twas me as asked the question.'

'Questions,' he said. 'And too many.'

Well! If that was the way of it, she'd not say another word … no, not one!

They sat in silence, listening to the wind whistling through cracks and crannies between the planks of the old brig. The cold was like weasels biting and the strong strange musky smell of the fo'c'sle played on her stomach that was already protesting over the gobbled bread. She hadn't intended speaking again, but curiosity nagged her – besides, talking would keep her mind off her queasy innards.

'Is this a slaver then? How many folks did it carry?' and when he refused to answer, added stiffly: 'Jess … that's what I'm called,' as a first move to soften him – and then remembered she was supposed to be a boy. Oh Christmas! But a nigger wouldn't know one name from another, would he? Anyway 'Jess' was near enough right for boy or girl.

There was no response, so she went on hastily: 'The Cap'n called thee Midnight. Is that all of th'name?'

'No.'

There was another long pause.

'Well, go on then, tell us the rest of it.'

'Why should I tell you anything?'

'I was only asking kindly like,' Jess said, nettled. 'Besides, th'know mine now, and I'll tell thee my trade like thee asked. 'Tis that of a smith.' It was near enough true. Hadn't she cleaned and swept for Samson long enough? She'd watched him working, learned the feel and way of shaping iron through eyes and ears and nose. She only lacked strength, that was all. Not that a girl would ever be allowed to touch the great hammers or take the white-hot metal from the furnace with the giant tongs. There was nothing for girls, only drudgery and breeding, specially paupers like herself.

Midnight had turned his head. His face was in darkness, but he must be looking at her. She looked down, afraid that the shirt and waistcoat had shaped themselves round her small breasts and so betrayed her.

'As for any home, I've none, nor never did have,' she said quickly to distract him from too much thinking. 'So now th'knows all, and owes me summat in return.'

He laughed then, and she was surprised. It was the first friendly sound that day; real and infectious. She found herself smiling.

'Perhaps I'll tell you one day, if we chance to get acquainted, but for the present my name is all I have that belongs to me alone,' he said.

Jess felt cheated. The warmth that had come with his laughter faded, and she felt he had tricked her into saying more than she intended. Absurdly, she felt hurt; the more so because she understood his feelings about his name. Sympathy and resentment jostled each other. The chain joining the handcuffs chinked and pulled at her wrist as he moved, and resentment won. To be chained like a common criminal and to a *nigger* – oh it was too much! Her earlier fears about what terrors lay in store returned, all the more powerful because for a few minutes she had forgotten them. But she wasn't going to show she was scared. Her mouth tightened. She would be silent as the grave this time – give her mind to getting free.

Marjorie Darke

TEXT LEVEL WORK

Comprehension

A 1 Where are Jess and Midnight sitting?

2 Where was Midnight living before he came to Bristol?

3 Name three products that merchants took to Africa to trade for slaves.

4 For whom, and where, did Jess work previously?

5 How does the reader know that Jess is a prisoner?

B 1 Explain the following in your own words:

a '*foreign way of leaning on the wrong part of the words*'

b '*cussing and blinding*'

c '*loading up the Guineamen*'.

2 What do you learn of the character of Midnight through Jess' impressions of him?

3 What do you learn from the following?

  a '*hoping for tales about unknown Africa*'
  b '*Like sunsets they were ... lovely!*'
  c '*Oh Christmas!*'

4 Using evidence from the text, explain why Jess is in a difficult situation.

C Using evidence from the text, what can you infer about the character of Jess? You should comment on:

- her attitude to Midnight
- her questions
- her hopes and fears.

WORD LEVEL WORK

Vocabulary

Dictionary and contextual work

Use a dictionary and the context of the passage to explain the meaning of the following words:

1 kegs	5 fetters	9 acquainted
2 fo'c'sle or forecastle	6 crannies	10 resentment
3 silhouetted	7 drudgery	11 tongs
4 smithy	8 paupers	12 indignity

Spelling

'dge' words

Key word: dru**dge**ry

1 Use the key word in a sentence of your own.

2 Learn these important 'dge' words:

  knowle**dge**   cartri**dge**   ju**dge**   bri**dge**

HINT

*Remember to drop the 'e' when adding a suffix beginning with a vowel eg ju**dge** – ju**dg**ing*

SENTENCE LEVEL WORK

Grammar and punctuation

Formality and informality

Formal language is more common in writing than in speech.
Most speech is informal or colloquial, ie everyday language.
Slang is a very informal use of language, eg

  man = formal
  guy = informal
  bloke = slang

To make informal language into formal language, you can use:

- passive voice – 'Many things may be done in order to ...'

- 'It' as the subject of the sentence – 'It is possible that ...'
- 'There' as the subject of the sentence – 'There is a little chance of ...'
- 'One' as the subject of the sentence ('One' is a formal way of saying 'You' plural) – 'One might think ...'.

Make these informal/slang examples into formal sentences.

1 That bloke Midnight treated the girl really nice.
2 Jess was stroppy when she was scared.
3 She was often hungry 'cos she couldn't get enough grub.
4 Jess acted like she was potty, to keep people away from her.
5 Do-gooders aren't tough enough on villains, they're too wishy-washy.
6 Jess wasn't chicken when the going got tough.
7 She thought that Samson was a real clot.
8 'You must be bonkers,' Jess shouted across the pub.
9 'I'm 'aving nothing to do with a slob, like you!'
10 'What're you gawping at?' Jess snarled.
11 She thought that he was acting naff, when he tried to help.
12 'I'll clobber 'im, if he comes near me,' she thought.

TEXT LEVEL WORK

Writing

Dialogue

The First of Midnight is a contemporary prose novel set in late eighteenth century Bristol. The central characters are a working-class Bristolian girl in her early teens and a gentlemanly and intelligent Negro slave in his late teens/early twenties.

Dialogue in prose fiction tries to seem 'natural' but it cannot be totally realistic.

Everyday conversation wanders off the point and is full of half-finished sentences, as well as 'ums' and 'ers'. On the other hand, we can't expect all characters to sound like professors of English. So, writers try to create conversations that *seem real*.

Language features

Dialogue

The writer uses dialogue to:

- reinforce the setting (time and place)
  - accents communicate a feeling of a particular time or place, eg

    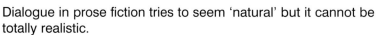
    '*So now th'knows all, and owes me summat in return.*'

Establish early on that a character has an accent then be very sparing with the use of it
- vocabulary is sometimes made up by the writer (especially in the fantasy/science fiction genres). Introduce new words gradually, making sure their meaning is clear, eg

  'fo'c'sle'

Even common words can be used differently; they can be put in italics for emphasis, eg

  'chained like a common criminal and to a *nigger*'

- use good dictionaries, such as *The Shorter Oxford Dictionary* or *The Penguin Dictionary of Historical Slang* to check the use of a historical word or slang, eg

  fo'c'sle or forecastle: n. (Hist.) short raised deck at the bow, (in warship later but now obs.) part of upper deck forward of aftermost fore-shroud: the forward part of a ship below the deck, traditionally used as the crew's living quarters.

If you can't date it or find it for the period you are writing about, don't use it
- avoid false 'olde worlde' words, such as 'Forsooth', 'Prithee', 'Egad'
- avoid modern slang and catchphrases like 'Get a life!'

- illuminate the characters
  - reality – make the conversations seem real and believable
  - verbal styles – people have individual variations in their speech, word-choice, syntax and accent but be consistent for each character
  - internal dialogue (a character thinking or 'talking' to him/herself) shows the characters' emotions, helping the reader to understand and share the emotions of the characters, eg

    'If that was the way of it, she'd not say another word … no, not one!'

  - modern attitudes – don't mix modern attitudes and beliefs with those of a different culture, time or place in the dialogue between characters

- advance the plot
  - avoid characters telling or reminding one another of something they should know already: in dialogue only give information that is necessary to the plot, eg

    'What'll the Cap'n do with me? How long do us have to stay here?'

Technical hints

- exclamation marks – use exclamation marks, in order to place emphasis, but not too often, eg

  'Like sunsets they were … lovely!'

- speech tags like 'he asked' or 'she said' are necessary, eg

  '"Thee his servant?" she asked.'

But don't use them all the time and don't go to the other extreme of trying to use masses of alternative ways of saying the same thing, eg

  *'What's to become of me?' Jess **ventured** to ask.'*

Writing assignment

Write a prose scene based in a different period of history from our own, which includes dialogue between characters. Use the information in the language features to help you check that you have reinforced the setting, illuminated the characters and advanced the plot.

The scene should include:

- two main characters trying to find out more about one another
- a balance of prose and dialogue
- dialogue that reveals very different attitudes to the situation they are in
- a particular place and a particular time that is not '*now*'
- a reason why the characters are there and why they need to find a way out of there
- an ending which leaves the situation unresolved.

cropped
like a sheep.

In this extract from the novel, Sons and Lovers, *by D H Lawrence, the author describes the relationship between Mr and Mrs Morel. Mr Morel is a coal miner, while his wife comes from a family that thought itself superior. In this passage, the writer outlines the power struggle for dominance that takes place between the husband and wife.*

Gertrude Morel was very ill when the boy was born. Morel was good to her, as good as gold. But she felt very lonely, miles away from her own people. She felt lonely with him now, and his presence only made it more intense.

The boy was small and frail at first, but he came on quickly. He was a beautiful child, with dark gold ringlets, and dark blue eyes, which changed gradually to a clear grey. His mother loved him passionately. He came just when her own bitterness of disillusion was hardest to bear; when her faith in life was shaken, and her soul felt dreary and lonely. She made much of the child, and the father was jealous.

At last Mrs Morel despised her husband. She turned to the child, she turned from the father. He had begun to neglect her; the novelty of his own home was gone. He had no grit, she said bitterly to herself. What he felt just at the minute, that was all to him. He could not abide by anything. There was nothing at the back of all his show.

There began a battle between the husband and wife, a fearful, bloody battle that ended only with the death of one. She fought to make him undertake his own responsibilities, to make him fulfil his obligations. But he was too different from her. His nature was purely sensuous, and she strove to make him moral, religious. She tried to force him to face things. He could not endure it – it drove him out of his mind.

While the baby was still tiny, the father's temper had become so irritable that it was not to be trusted. The child had only to give a little trouble, when the man began to bully. A little more, and the hard hands of the collier hit the baby. Then Mrs Morel loathed her husband, loathed him for days: and he went out and drank: and she cared very little what he did. Only, on his return, she scathed him with her satire.

The estrangement between them caused him, knowingly or unknowingly, grossly to offend her where he would not have done.

... William was only one year old, and his mother was proud of him, he was so pretty. She was not well off now, but her sisters kept the boy in clothes. Then, with his little white hat curled with an ostrich feather, and his white coat, he was a joy to her, the twining wisps of hair clustering round his head. Mrs Morel lay listening, one Sunday morning, to the chatter of the father and child downstairs. Then she dozed off. When she came downstairs, a great fire glowed in the grate, the room was hot, the breakfast was roughly laid. And seated in his armchair, against the chimney piece, sat Morel, rather timid: and standing between his legs, the child – cropped like a sheep, with such an odd round poll – looking wondering at her: and on a newspaper spread out upon the hearth rug, a myriad of crescent-shaped curls, like the petals of a marigold scattered in the reddening firelight.

Mrs Morel stood still. It was her first baby. She went very white, and was unable to speak.

'What dost think o' 'im?' Morel laughed uneasily.

She gripped her two fists, lifted them, and came forward. Morel shrank back.

'I could kill you, I could!' she said. She choked with rage, her two fists uplifted.

'Yer non want ter make a wench on 'im,' Morel said, in a frightened tone, bending his head to shield his eyes from hers. His attempt at laughter had vanished.

The mother looked down at the jagged, close clipped head of her child. She put her hands on his hair, and stroked and fondled his head.

'Oh – my boy!' she faltered. Her lip trembled, her face broke, and, snatching up the child, she buried her face in his shoulder and cried painfully. She was one of those women who cannot cry: whom it hurts as it hurts a man. It was like ripping something out of her, her sobbing. Morel sat with his elbows on his knees, his hands gripped together till the knuckles were white. He gazed in the fire, feeling almost stunned, as if he could not breathe.

Presently she came to an end, soothed the child –

and cleared away the breakfast table. She left the newspaper, littered with curls, spread upon the hearthrug. At last her husband gathered it up and put it at the back of the fire. She went about her work with closed mouth and very quiet. Morel was subdued. He crept about wretchedly, and his meals were a misery that day. She spoke to him civilly, and never alluded to what he had done. But he felt something final had happened.

Afterwards, she said she had been silly, that the boy's hair would have had to be cut, sooner or later. In the end, she even brought herself to say to her husband, it was just as well he had played barber when he did. But she knew, and Morel knew, that that act had caused something momentous to take place in her soul. She remembered the scene all her life, as one in which she had suffered the most intensely.

This act of masculine clumsiness was the spear through the side of her love for Morel. Before, while she had striven against him bitterly, she had fretted after him, as if he had gone astray from her. Now she ceased to fret for his love: he was an outsider to her. This made life much more bearable.

Nevertheless, she still continued to strive with him. She still had her high moral sense, inherited from generations of Puritans. It was now a religious instinct, and she was almost a fanatic with him, because she loved him, or had loved him. If he sinned, she tortured him. If he drank, and lied, was often a poltroon, sometimes a knave, she wielded the lash unmercifully.

D H Lawrence

TEXT LEVEL WORK

Comprehension

A 1 What is Mrs Morel's Christian name?

2 What is the name of Mrs Morel's son?

3 On which day of the week did Mr Morel cut his son's hair?

4 How old was the son when his hair was cut?

5 What colour were the son's hair and eyes?

B 1 Explain the following in your own words:

a '*He had no grit ...*'
b '*... she scathed him with her satire.*'
c '*... with such an odd round poll ...*'.

2 What do you learn of the character of Morel from the passage?

3 What do you learn from the following:

a '*She turned to the child, she turned from the father.*'
b '*... her sisters kept the boy in clothes.*'
c '*... that act had caused something momentous to take place in her soul*'?

4 Using evidence from the text, show how Mr Morel and his wife make some efforts to 'patch things up' between them. How do we know that they feel their efforts are doomed?

C Using evidence from the text, what can you infer about the differences in character of Mr and Mrs Morel? You should comment on their:

- backgrounds
- attitudes
- behaviour.

WORD LEVEL WORK

Vocabulary

Dictionary and contextual work

Use a dictionary and the context of the passage to explain the meaning of the following words:

1 novelty	5 estrangement	9 fret
2 obligations	6 myriad	10 moral
3 sensuous	7 crescent	11 fanatic
4 collier	8 alluded	12 poltroon

Spelling

'ought' words

Key words: **fought**   br**ought**   th**ought**

1 Use the key words in sentences of your own.
2 Learn these important 'ought' words:

n**ought**   **ought**   s**ought**

HINT

Look out for 'aught' words which make the same sound, eg 'daughter'

SENTENCE LEVEL WORK

Grammar and punctuation

Active and passive voice

When the subject does the action of the verb, it is called the **active voice**, eg

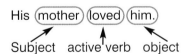

His (mother) (loved) (him.)

Subject   active verb   object

When the subject is the receiver of the action of the verb, it is called the **passive voice**, eg

The (baby) (was hit) by his (father.)

Subject   passive verb   object

Copy and complete the table. State whether the sentences are in the active or passive voice.

Sentence	Active/Passive
Her faith was shaken.	
Mrs Morel despised her husband.	
He went out and drank.	
The breakfast was roughly laid.	
Against the chimney piece, sat Morel.	
The boy was born.	
He was loved by his mother.	
He gazed in the fire.	
Morel was scathed by her satire.	
She wielded the lash unmercifully.	

TEXT LEVEL WORK

Writing

Dialogue

Sons and Lovers is a prose novel set in a Nottinghamshire mining community. The central characters are a working-class miner and his wife, who comes from a family of higher social status than her husband.

Dialogue in prose fiction tries to seem 'natural' but it cannot be totally realistic. Everyday conversation wanders off the point and is full of half-finished sentences, as well as 'ums' and 'ers'. On the other hand, we can't expect all characters to sound like elaborate, scholarly, professors of English. So, writers try to create conversations that *seem real*.

Language features

Formal and informal language

New words and phrases are used in spoken or informal language sooner than in formal, written language. Most languages have a standard form; it's the form of the language used in government, education and other formal contexts. But standard English is just one dialect of English.

Dialect

- Every dialect of every language has rules. For example:

  1 I didn't eat any breakfast.
  2 I didn't eat no breakfast.

  Sentence 1 follows the rules of standard English; sentence 2 follows a set of rules used in some dialects. To make a negative sentence, in 1, 'breakfast' is marked as negative by using the word 'any'; in 2, it's shown to be negative by using 'no'. Sentences like 2 only sound 'wrong' if you happened to grow up speaking a dialect that doesn't use them.

- You may have been taught to avoid 'splitting infinitives', as in 3:

  3 I was asked to thoroughly water the houseplants.

  This is said to be 'ungrammatical' because 'thoroughly' splits the infinitive 'to water'. Why are split infinitives considered to be so bad? Because seventeenth century scholars believed Latin to be the ideal language. In Latin, an infinitive like 'to water' is a single word; it's impossible to split it up. So today, 300 years later, we're still being taught that sentences like 3 are wrong, because someone in the 1600s thought English should be more like Latin.

- Here's one last example. Over the past few decades, three new ways of reporting speech have appeared:

  4 So Tamara goes, 'Hey – I wish I'd been there!'

  5 So Tamara is like, 'Hey – I wish I'd been there!'

  In 4, 'goes' means the same thing as 'said', and it is reporting Tamara's actual words. In 5, 'is like' means the speaker is telling us more or less what Tamara said. If Tamara had used different words for the same idea, 5 would be suitable, but 4 would not.

Punctuation of dialogue to show dialect

When trying to suggest a dialect, with an accent, writers sometimes spell words phonetically (how they sound). The writer is indicating how the words should be said by the character who has a particular dialect or accent, eg

'"What dost think o' 'im?" Morel laughed uneasily.'

The spelling of the word 'dost', meaning 'do', shows that Mr Morel speaks in the dialect of a Nottingham miner. The phrase 'o' 'im' is written with apostrophes to indicate that words have been contracted or shortened to show the effects of Morel's dialect on his accent.

Grammar also changes, according to dialect, and this is shown by the word order, as well as by phonetic spelling and the use of apostrophes to show contraction, eg

'"Yer non want ter make a wench on 'im," Morel said.'

In this example, instead of saying 'You do not want', the writer said 'Yer non want'. Instead of spelling 'to make' in formal standard English, D H Lawrence wrote 'ter make', to show Morel's pronunciation. Rather than saying 'to make a girl of him', Lawrence wrote 'a wench on 'im'. The writer has used a dialect word, 'wench', for 'girl', and the word 'on' for 'of'. He has used an apostrophe of contraction on the word 'him', to make it ''im'.

Writing assignment

Write a prose scene, which includes dialogue between characters. Use the information in the language features to help you check that you have shown the difference between informal and formal language.

The scene should include:

- formal and informal language
- a balance of prose and dialogue
- two main characters whose dialogue reveals that they have very different attitudes to the situation they are in
- two main characters whose dialogue reveals that they have very different dialects
- dialects or accents that are from a particular place
- phonetic spelling, grammar and the use of apostrophes to show contractions that are suitable to the characters' dialects and accents.

send out
a dove.

King Pelias is warned by an oracle that his death will come at the hands of a man with one bare foot. Very soon, Jason arrives for the banquet Pelias is giving in honour of his father Poseidon, having lost one of his sandals in the river. Pelias decides to send Jason on a perilous voyage to steal the Golden Fleece of a sacred winged ram which hung in a grove sacred to the goddess Athene and was guarded by a dragon.

After various adventures on their voyage the Argonauts meet Phineus, an old man, who warns them of the danger ahead.

'When you leave me, the first thing you see will be the two Cyanean Rocks, at the end of the straits. To the best of my knowledge, no one has ever made his way between them, for not being fixed to the bottom of the sea, they frequently collide, flinging up the water in a seething mass which falls on the rocky flanks of the straits with a resounding roar. Now if, as I take it, you are god-fearing travellers and men of sense, you will be advised by me: you will not rashly throw away your lives or rush into danger with the recklessness of youth. Make an experiment first. Send out a dove from the *Argo* to explore the way. If she succeeds in flying in between the Rocks and out across the sea, do not hesitate to follow in her path, but get a firm grip on your oars and cleave the water of the straits. For that is the time when salvation will depend, not on your prayers, but on your strength of arm. So think of nothing else, be firm, and spend your energies on what will pay you best. By all means pray to the gods, but choose an earlier moment. And if the dove flies on, but comes to grief midway, turn back. It is always better to submit to Heaven; and you could not possibly escape a dreadful end. The Rocks would crush you, even if the *Argo* were an iron ship.

After leaving the old man, Jason and the Argonauts come upon the Clashing Rocks, just as he had predicted.

In due course they found themselves entering the narrowest part of the winding straits. Rugged cliffs hemmed them in on either side, and the *Argo* as she advanced began to feel a swirling undercurrent. They moved ahead in fear, for now the clash of the colliding Rocks and the thunder of surf on the shores fell ceaselessly on their ears. Euphemus seized the dove and climbed on to the prow, while the oarsmen, at Tiphys' orders, made a special effort, hoping by their own strength of arm to drive *Argo* through the Rocks forthwith. They rounded a bend and saw a thing that no one after them has seen – the Rocks were moving apart. Their hearts sank; but now Euphemus launched the dove on her flight and the eyes of all were raised to watch her as she passed between the Rocks.

Once more the Rocks met face to face with a resounding crash, flinging a great cloud of spray into the air. The sea gave a terrific roar and the broad sky rang again. Caverns underneath the crags bellowed as the sea came surging in. A great wave broke against the cliffs and the white foam swept high above them. *Argo* was spun around as the flood reached her.

But the dove got through, unscathed but for the tips of her tail-feathers, which were nipped off by the Rocks. The oarsmen gave a cry of triumph and Tiphys shouted at them to row with all their might, for the Rocks were opening again. So they rowed on full of dread, till the backwash, overtaking them, thrust the *Argo* in between the Rocks. Then the fears of all were turned to panic. Sheer destruction hung above their heads.

They had already reached a point where they could see the vast sea opening out on either side, when they were suddenly faced by a tremendous billow arched like an overhanging rock. They bent their heads down at the sight, for it seemed about to fall and overwhelm the ship. But Tiphys just in time checked her as she plunged forward, and the great wave slid under her keel. Indeed it raised her stern so high in the air that she was carried clear of the Rocks. Euphemus ran along shouting to all his friends to put their backs into their rowing, and with answering shouts they struck the water. Yet for every foot that *Argo* made she lost two, though the oars bent like curved bows as the men put out their strength.

... This was the moment when Athene intervened. Holding on to the hard rock with her left hand, she pushed the ship through with the other; and *Argo* clove the air like a winged arrow, though even so the Rocks, clashing in their accustomed way, sheared off the tip of the mascot on the stern. When the men had thus got through unhurt, Athene soared up to Olympus. But the Rocks were now rooted for ever in one spot close to one another. It had been decided by the happy gods that this should be their fate when a human being had seen them and sailed through. The Argonauts, freed from the cold grip of panic, breathed again when they saw the sky once more and the vast ocean stretching out ahead. They felt that they had come through Hell alive.

Tiphys was the first to speak. 'I think' he said, 'that we can say all's well. *Argo* is safe and so are we. And for that, to whom are we indebted but Athene, who endowed the ship with supernatural strength when Argus drove the bolts home in her planks? *Argo* shall not be caught; that seems to be a law. And so, Lord Jason, now that Heaven has allowed us to pass safely through the Rocks, I beg you not to dread so much the duty that your king assigned you. Has not Phineus told us that from now on we shall meet no obstacle we cannot easily surmount?'

Tiphys, with that, steered straight across the open sea along the Bithynian coast. But Jason, for his own purposes, took him gently to task. 'Tiphys,' he said, 'why do you try to comfort me in my distress? I was blind and made a fatal error. When Pelias ordered me to undertake this mission, I ought to have refused outright, even though he would have torn me limb from limb without compunction. But as things are, I am obsessed by fears and intolerable anxiety, hating the thought of the cruel sea that we must cross and of what may happen when we land and find the natives hostile, as we are sure to do at every point. Ever since you all rallied to my side these cares have occupied my mind, and when each day is done I spend the night in misery. It is easy for you, Tiphys, to talk in a cheerful vein. You are only concerned for your own life, whereas I care nothing for mine, but *am* concerned for each and all alike, you and the rest of my friends. How can I tell whether I shall bring you safely back to Hellas?'

from *The Voyage of Argo*
by Apollonius Of Rhodes,
translated by E V Rieu

TEXT LEVEL WORK

Comprehension

A 1 Who warns Jason and the Argonauts of the danger of the Cyanean Rocks?

2 Why were the Cyanean Rocks a danger to the Argonauts?

3 Quote from the text to explain what happened when the dove was launched by Euphemus towards the Rocks.

4 Who intervened to help the Argonauts?

5 Even though they had braved the Rocks and come through safely, why was Jason still troubled?

B 1 Explain the following in your own words:

   a *'To the best of my knowledge ...'*
   b *'... comes to grief ...'*
   c *'... their hearts sank.'*

  2 What do you learn of the character of the Argonauts through Phineus' impression of them?

  3 How does the author build up the tension as the *Argo* approaches the Rocks by appealing to the senses of sight and hearing?

  4 Using evidence from the text, show the differing attitudes of the gods to the world of men.

C Using evidence from the text what can you infer about the character of Jason? You should comment on:

- his attitude to Phineus
- his relationship with the Argonauts
- his acceptance of the mission
- his attitude to the Argonauts.

WORD LEVEL WORK

Vocabulary

Dictionary and contextual work
Use a dictionary and the context of the passage to explain the meaning of the following words:

1 perilous	5 salvation	9 endowed
2 collide	6 forthwith	10 assigned
3 recklessness	7 unscathed	11 compunction
4 cleave	8 intervened	12 intolerable

Spelling

'ent' words
Key words: experim**ent**   mom**ent**   undercurr**ent**

  1 Use these key words in sentences of your own.
  2 Learn these important 'ent' words:

    compon**ent**   ingredi**ent**   cont**ent**   elem**ent**
    nutri**ent**   repres**ent**   pati**ent**

> *HINT*
>
> If a word ends in 'ent' it is likely to take 'ence', eg pati**ent** – pati**ence**

SENTENCE LEVEL WORK

Grammar and punctuation

Sentences and fragments

> Sentences can become complicated and confused. This often happens when they consist of both independent and dependent clauses. The wrong use of dependent clauses can result in incomplete sentences.

Often, you can spot incomplete sentences by looking for:
- phrases starting with prepositions, eg 'after', 'between', 'near', 'under'
- verbs ending with 'ing', eg

  'After the Argonauts passed the rocks, the crew celebrated. Danc**ing** on the deck.'
- 'wh' words, eg 'who', 'which', 'when', 'where'
- sentences or phrases beginning with 'to', eg

  'Tiphys released the dove. **To** show the way through the rocks.'

Copy these sentences. Underline the independent clauses in red and the dependent clauses in blue. Circle the words that indicate that there is a dependent clause, eg

Tiphys released the dove (to) show the way through the rocks.

1 They entered the narrow straits, which were bordered by cliffs.
2 As she advanced, *Argo* was seized by undercurrents.
3 Seizing a dove, Euphemus climbed on the prow.
4 Since the dove passed the rocks, the oarsmen redoubled their efforts.
5 Though they were terrified, the Argonauts breathed again.
6 The goddess, Athene, who guarded them, helped *Argo* through the gap.
7 The rocks, which had been moving, were now rooted in one spot.
8 Tiphys was first to speak, saying that they were safe.
9 Jason was fearful, hating the cruel sea.
10 Throughout the voyage, Jason worried about his men's safety.

TEXT LEVEL WORK

Writing

Viewpoint

The extract from *Jason and the Argonauts* is a narrative piece of writing told from the viewpoint of the 'anonymous' narrator. He is not involved in the situation but relates what is happening.

Language features

Viewpoint

The **third person** is used when the story is narrated by someone who is not a character in the story. The viewpoint is that of the narrator and is written in the third person, eg

'In due course **they** found themselves ...';
'... **she** pushed the ship through with the other ...'.

If the incident had been related by one of the characters in the story, it would have been written in the first person, eg

- one of the Argonauts: 'In due course **we** found ourselves ...'
- Athene: '... **I** pushed the ship through with the other ...'.

Descriptive language

The story of *Jason and the Argonauts* is essentially an adventure story where the characters are beset by danger. The reader must be able to 'experience' the danger through the descriptive writing, using powerful verbs and vivid adjectives. Which is more convincing of the perilous situation the Argonauts find themselves in:

- '*swirling undercurrent*' or 'the water was a bit rough'?
- '*the clash of the colliding Rocks*' or 'the Rocks bumped each other'?

Dominant impression

The dominant impression created by the writer changes:

- a sense of tension as the *Argo* approaches the clashing Rocks and attempts to get through, culminating in the desperate situation when we read:

  '*Yet for every foot that Argo made she lost two ...*'

  Will they make it?

- a sense of relief when Athene intervenes:

  '*Holding on to the hard rock with her left hand, she pushed the ship through with the other ...*'

  Against all the odds, the ship has come through relatively unscathed.

- a sense of foreboding

  Despite the relief at the success of getting through the Rocks, the reader is left with a sense of more dangers to come as Jason admits:

  '*I am obsessed by fears and intolerable anxiety ...*'

  Have the Argonauts survived one dangerous situation only to be overcome by the next? Will their quest be successful or will they perish?

Writing assignment

Change the viewpoint

Imagine that you are either Jason or Athene and relate the incident of the Clashing Rocks from your viewpoint beginning when the *Argo* enters '*the narrowest part of the winding straits*'.

Remember:

- use the first person
- choose your vocabulary carefully to convey the danger of the situation
- include your thoughts and feelings as the incident unfolds.

Personal choice

Choose one of the following assignments.

1 Imagine you are Jason. The *Argo* is built and now you have to advertise for a crew. The advertisement is designed to inform and persuade and must include:

- details of the quest ensuring that anyone who applies to join the crew is aware of the dangers and the promise of reward
- the qualities you are looking for in a fellow Argonaut.

2 The quest has been successfully completed. Write an interview with Jason which centres on the incident of the Clashing Rocks.

Home Thoughts from Abroad

Oh, to be in England
Now that April's there,
And whoever wakes in England
Sees, some morning, unaware,
That the lowest boughs and the brushwood sheaf
Round the elm-tree bole are in tiny leaf,
While the chaffinch sings on the orchard bough
In England – now!

And after April, when May follows,
And the whitethroat builds, and all the swallows!
Hark, where my blossomed pear-tree in the hedge
Leans to the field and scatters on the clover
Blossoms and dewdrops – at the bent spray's edge –
That's the wise thrush; he sings each song twice over,
Lest you should think he never could recapture
The first fine careless rapture!
And though the fields look rough with hoary dew
All will be gay when noontide wakes anew
The buttercups, the little children's dower
– Far brighter than this gaudy melon-flower!

Robert Browning

Homeward Bound

I'm sitting in a railway station,
Got a ticket for my destination.
On a tour of one night stands
   my suitcase and guitar in hand
And ev'ry stop is neatly planned
   for a poet and a one man band.
Homeward Bound.
I wish I was.
Homeward Bound.

Home where my thought's escaping,
Home where my music's playing,
Home where my love lies waiting
Silently for me.

Ev'ry day's an endless stream
Of cigarettes and magazines.
And each town looks the same to me,
   the movies and the factories
And ev'ry stranger's face I see
   reminds me that I long to be,
Homeward Bound.
I wish I was.
Homeward Bound.

Home where my thought's escaping,
Home where my music's playing,
Home where my love lies waiting
Silently for me.

Though I'll sing my songs again,
I'll play the game and pretend.
But all my words come back to me
   in shades of mediocrity
Like emptiness in harmony
   I need someone to comfort me.
Homeward Bound.
I wish I was.
Homeward Bound.

Home where my thought's escaping,
Home where my music's playing,
Home where my love lies waiting
Silently for me.

Paul Simon

TEXT LEVEL WORK

Comprehension

A *Home Thoughts from Abroad*

1 In what month does the poet long '*to be in England*'?

2 What two signs of the month does the poet especially remember?

3 Why, according to the poet, does the '*wise thrush*' sing '*each song twice over*'?

Homeward Bound

4 Where is the poet when he is thinking about home?

5 What does the poet imagine is happening at home?

6 What reminds the poet of how much he longs to be at home?

B *Home Thoughts from Abroad*

1 What sort of area in England do you think the poet comes from?

2 Do you think the poet's memories of England are reliable and comprehensive?

Homeward Bound

3 Find at least three 'clues' in the poem to support the theory that the poet is a singer-songwriter.

4 What do you think is the poet's state of mind? Quote evidence from the poem to support your answer.

C Compare and contrast the two poems. You should include:

• each poet's attitude to being away from home
• the physical setting each poet describes
• the verse structure and how it reflects the 'mood' of the poem.

WORD LEVEL WORK

Vocabulary

Dictionary and contextual work

Use a dictionary and the context of the extract to explain the meaning of the following words.

Home Thoughts from Abroad	*Homeward Bound*
1 unaware	6 destination
2 bole	7 neatly
3 lest	8 stream
4 rapture	9 mediocrity
5 hoary	10 harmony

Spelling

'ture' words

Key words: recap**ture**   rap**ture**

1 Use these key words in sentences of your own.
2 Learn these important 'ture' words:

agricul**ture**   tempera**ture**   tex**ture**

infrastruc**ture**   manufac**ture**

SENTENCE LEVEL WORK

Grammar and punctuation

Sentences and fragments

An incomplete sentence is sometimes called a **sentence fragment**. It is only part of a sentence, missing out a subject or a verb. Usually, sentence fragments are easy to correct:

- add the fragment to the sentence that comes before or after
- add the missing subject, verb or clause to complete the sentence.

Better still, avoid writing sentence fragments by being aware of what is likely to produce them:

- missing subjects, eg 'Shouting in the streets.' This sentence does not say *who* is shouting in the streets
- starting with prepositions, eg 'In a brand new house overlooking the park.'
- '-ing' words. These '-ing' verbs are not complete verbs. They need helpers, known as auxiliary verbs, to make them complete, eg 'The man sing**ing**.' This sentence has a subject, 'man', and a verb, 'singing'. The verb is incomplete and needs an auxiliary verb to help complete it, ie, '**is** singing'
- clauses beginning with 'to', eg '**To** go home.' This sentence requires an independent clause to be added to the dependent clause, eg 'To go home was all he wished for.'

Explain whether the following sentence fragments are missing punctuation, a subject, a verb or a clause. Then, modify the sentence fragments so that they become complete sentences.

1 I am taking Italian classes. To help me on holiday.
2 Chantal went shopping. To get her mind off her music exam.
3 Next week we will visit our favourite instructor. Who helped us pass our driving test.
4 Although Ben did all his preparations. He still failed his driving test.
5 When Sonia picked up the slimy frog.
6 Which led to violence and general unpleasantness.
7 Reading chapter after chapter in the textbook.

8 Even though I liked art.
9 To face up to her responsibilities.
10 Such as French, History and Psychology.

TEXT LEVEL WORK

Writing

Poetic form

> Both the poems, *Home Thoughts from Abroad* and *Homeward Bound*, have the same theme – longing for home – but are very different in how each poet explores this theme.

Language features

Verse structure

Poets often choose the verse structure of their poems, ie number and length of verses, to reflect what they are writing about.

Home Thoughts from Abroad

- In this poem there is a short first verse beginning with four short lines as if this memory has suddenly burst upon the poet's mind. The next four lines are longer and more descriptive, reflecting the poet conjuring up the memories of England in his mind's eye.

- The second verse continues this style as the poet brings to mind more and more detail.

Homeward Bound

- The verse structure here is very different. On the page it looks like the '*endless stream*' the poet refers to.

- Each verse opens with two short lines, showing the poet has no real interest in where he is and what he is doing.

- The next two lines of each verse are much longer, ideas and sensations almost crowding into each other, reflecting the poet's frustration at his situation.

- The chorus is repeated at the end of each verse to emphasise his need and longing to be home.

Rhythm and rhyme

Home Thoughts from Abroad

- The rhythm is not regular, perhaps reflecting the rather random nature of the memories.

- The rhyme follows a similar irregular pattern.

Homeward Bound

- Each verse follows the same rhythm pattern which encourages the reader to speed up as the poet describes the unpleasant details of his situation.

- Similarly, the rhyme scheme is repeated in each verse:
  - lines 1 and 2 rhyme, eg 'station'/'destination'
  - lines 3 and 4 rhyme but a sense of urgency is created by these lines having half rhymes, eg 'stands'/'hands' / 'planned'/'band'.

Vocabulary choices

This is the most obvious way a poet conveys his feelings towards the theme.

Home Thoughts from Abroad

- The vocabulary is positive and uplifting, eg
  'sings'/'blossomed'/'rapture'/'gay'.

Homeward Bound

- In contrast the vocabulary choices here are negative and sombre, eg
  'one night stands'/'endless'/'looks the same to me'/'stranger's face'/
  'mediocrity'/'emptiness'.

Writing assignment

Write your own 'memories of home' poem. You should:

- follow the verse form and rhyme scheme of either *Home Thoughts from Abroad* or *Homeward Bound*

- decide whether you are unhappy at being away from home or relieved, and choose your vocabulary accordingly.

Personal choice

Choose one of the following assignments.

1 Imagine you are a singer-songwriter who experiences much the same situation as Paul Simon but enjoys the travelling and new experiences. Write a letter home to describe:

  - what you have been doing
  - what you have seen
  - your thoughts and feelings.

2 Imagine you are Robert Browning and the place you are in is in total contrast to the memories he recalls of England. Write a description of your present situation.

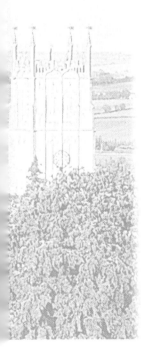

A cold coming we had of it.

'A cold coming we had of it,
Just the worst time of the year
For a journey, and such a long journey:
The ways deep and the weather sharp,
The very dead of winter.'   5
And the camels galled, sore-footed, refractory,
Lying down in the melting snow.
There were times we regretted
The summer palaces on slopes, the terraces,
And the silken girls bringing sherbet.   10
Then the camel men cursing and grumbling
And running away, and wanting their liquor and women,
And the night-fires going out, and the lack of shelters,
And the cities hostile and the towns unfriendly
And the villages dirty and charging high prices: 15
A hard time we had of it.
At the end we preferred to travel all night,
Sleeping in snatches,
With the voices singing in our ears, saying
That this was all folly.   20

Then at dawn we came down to a temperate valley,
Wet, below the snow line, smelling of vegetation,
With a running stream and a water-mill beating the darkness,
And three trees on the low sky.
And an old white horse galloped away in the meadow.   25
Then we came to a tavern with vine-leaves over the lintel,
Six hands at an open door dicing for pieces of silver,
And feet kicking the empty wine-skins.
But there was no information, and so we continued
And arriving at evening, not a moment too soon   30
Finding the place; it was (you may say) satisfactory.

All this was a long time ago, I remember,
And I would do it again, but set down
This set down
This: were we led all that way for   35
Birth or Death? There was a Birth, certainly,
We had evidence and no doubt. I had seen birth and death,
But had thought they were different; this Birth was
Hard and bitter agony for us, like Death, our death.
We returned to our places, these Kingdoms,   40
But no longer at ease here, in the old dispensation,
With an alien people clutching their gods.
I should be glad of another death.

T S Eliot

TEXT LEVEL WORK

Comprehension

A 1 In what season of the year does the journey take place?

2 By what means did the travellers make their journey?

3 Where did the travellers stop to try to find '*information*'?

4 When did they arrive at the place they were seeking?

5 What were the travellers certain they had witnessed?

B 1 Explain the following in your own words:

a '*There were times we regretted
The summer palaces on slopes ...*'
b '*That this was all folly.*'
c '*... set down this ...*'.

2 What impression does the poet create in lines 12 to 15 with '*And ... and ...*'?

3 The poet uses short lines in the first stanza and longer more 'flowing' lines in the second stanza. Why do you think he changes the style in this way?

4 What '*birth*' do you think the travellers had witnessed and in what way had the travellers seen their own death?

C Explain how the poet uses contrast in the poem and what effect this has on the reader.

You should consider:

• the weather
• the travellers' home and their journey
• the travellers' attitude to their home during and after the journey.

WORD LEVEL WORK

Vocabulary

Dictionary and contextual work

Use a dictionary and the context of the extract to explain the meaning of the following words:

1	galled	5	snatches	9	dispensation
2	refractory	6	temperate	10	alien
3	sherbert	7	lintel		
4	hostile	8	dicing		

Spelling

'ea' saying short 'e'

Key words: w**ea**ther   d**ea**d   m**ea**dow

1 Use these key words in sentences of your own.

2 Learn these important 'ea' saying short 'e' words:

inst**ea**d   m**ea**nt   ah**ea**d

SENTENCE LEVEL WORK

Grammar and punctuation

Relative clauses

Remember. A **main clause** (or simple sentence) has at least a subject and a verb, making a complete thought, eg

'The (Magi) (travelled).'
       \   \
    subject   verb

A **relative clause** tells us which thing or person is being talked about. It can also give us more information about a person or thing that has already been identified, eg

'People (who are wise) should be valued.'
           \
     relative clause

A relative clause does not make a complete thought. In the example above, 'who are wise' is not a complete thought and cannot stand alone.

Relative clauses begin with relative pronouns ('who', 'whoever', 'whom', 'whomever', 'which' or 'that') or relative adverbs ('when' or 'where'), eg

'(whom) the (Magi) (had travelled) so far to see'
    \   \   \
relative pronoun   subject   verb

Choose phrases from each column to form five complete sentences, each with a relative clause.

The camels	only slept in snatches.	There was a tavern
who preferred to travel at night	The Magi	lay down in the snow.
before returning home.	arrived in the evening.	The Magi
near a stream and a water-mill.	which were being difficult	when they reached their destination
who had travelled a long way	They witnessed a birth	which stood in a temperate valley

TEXT LEVEL WORK

Writing

Free verse

> *Journey of the Magi* is an example of free verse, which means it does not have:
>
> - regular stanzas
> - rhyme
> - regular rhythm (metre).
>
> The poet has written 'freely' without any of these constraints.

Language features

Structure

The structure of the poem is decided, not by having three stanzas of equal length, but by the stages of the journey and how much, or little, the poet needs to say about each stage:

- stanza 1: the journey itself through the harsh weather
- stanza 2: arriving at their destination
- stanza 3: the narrator reflecting on the journey.

Conversational style

The poet has written the poem in a conversational style. The reader can imagine him recalling the event in response to someone's questions, eg

- What was the journey like?
- Why did you go?
- What did you find?
- What do you think it meant?

Rhythm

Although free verse does not have a regular rhythm, eg de-da, de-da, de-da, de-da, a poet can, by careful choice of words, create a rhythmical feeling within the poem. Eliot does this in a variety of ways:

- alliteration:
    *'The **s**ummer palaces on **s**lopes, the terraces
    And the **s**ilken girls bringing **s**herbet.'*

- balance:
  '*The ways deep and the weather sharp.*'
- repetition:
  '*Just the worse time of year*
  *For a **journey**, and such a long **journey**.*'
- adjectival lists:
  '*And the camels **galled**, **sore-footed**, **refractory***'
- present participles:
  '*curs**ing**'/'grumbl**ing**'/'runn**ing**'/'want**ing***'.

Contrast

Through contrast the reader appreciates:

- the misery of the journey compared with the relief at arriving
- the misery of the journey compared with the memories of home
- how the attitude to home forever changes because of the journey.

Writing assignment

Think of an experience or imagine one where:

- you had to undertake a difficult journey
- what you discovered at your destination changed your life forever.

Write the experience in the form of free verse following the structure of
Journey of the Magi:

- stanza 1: the journey
- stanza 2: arriving
- stanza 3: reflection.

Each stanza only has to be as long as you need it to be. Although the poem
does not have to rhyme or have a strict rhythm, try to include some of Eliot's
techniques for creating a sense of rhythm within the poem.

Personal choice

Choose one of the following assignments.

1 Imagine you were one of the men looking after the camels.
   Write an account of the journey from your viewpoint.
   Remember:

   - the only reason you undertook the journey was because you had
     no choice
   - you had no idea why your master was undertaking the journey
   - decide whether witnessing the 'birth' had any effect on you
   - explain how you felt when you returned home.

2 Write a conversation between you as the narrator of the poem and one
   of the other Magi. The journey is hard and the weather terrible. Your
   companion wants to give up and go home. You want to carry on.

...kind
keepers.

In Shakespeare's play, The Tempest, *Prospero (the Duke of Milan) has been abandoned on a desert island by his brother, Antonio. A powerful magician, he survives and controls his environment. He causes a storm to shipwreck his enemies and bring them to the island. In this scene, he uses magic to trick his enemies, Antonio and Alonso (the King of Naples) into coming to him. Shakespeare mixes reality and illusion.*

O

Act III, Scene 3

Enter PROSPERO above, invisible. Enter several strange Shapes, bringing in a banquet; they dance about it with gentle actions of salutation; and, inviting the King, & c. to eat, they depart

ALONSO
    Give us kind keepers, heavens!
    What were these?
SEBASTIAN
    A living drollery. Now I will believe
    That there are unicorns; that in Arabia
    There is one tree, the phoenix' throne; one
        phoenix
    At this hour reigning there.
ANTONIO
    I'll believe both;
    And what does else want credit, come to me,
    And I'll be sworn 'tis true: travellers ne'er
        did lie,
    Though fools at home condemn them.
GONZALO
    If in Naples
    I should report this now, would they believe me?
    If I should say, I saw such islanders –
    For, certes, these are people of the island –
    Who, though they are of monstrous shape, yet,
        note,
    Their manners are more gentle-kind than of
    Our human generation you shall find
    Many, nay, almost any.
PROSPERO [*Aside*]
    Honest lord,
    Thou hast said well; for some of you there
        present
    Are worse than devils.

ALONSO
    I cannot too much muse
    Such shapes, such gesture and such sound,
        expressing –
    Although they want the use of tongue – a kind
    Of excellent dumb discourse.
PROSPERO [*Aside*]
    Praise in departing.
FRANCISCO
    They vanish'd strangely.
SEBASTIAN
    No matter, since
    They have left their viands behind; for we have
        stomachs. –
    Will't please you taste of what is here?
ALONSO
    Not I.
GONZALO
    Faith, sir, you need not fear. When we were
        boys,
    Who would believe that there were mountaineers
    Dewlapp'd like bulls, whose throats had hanging
        at them
    Wallets of flesh? or that there were such men
    Whose heads stood in their breasts? which now
        we find
    Each putter-out of five for one will bring us
    Good warrant of.
ALONSO
    I will stand to, and feed,
    Although my last; no matter, since I feel
    The best is past. – Brother, my lord the duke,
    Stand to and do as we.

Thunder and lightning. Enter ARIEL, like a harpy; claps his wings upon the table; and, with a quaint device, the banquet vanishes

ARIEL
    You are three men of sin, whom Destiny,
    That hath to instrument this lower world
    And what is in't, the never-surfeited sea
    Hath caused to belch up you; and on this island
    Where man doth not inhabit; you 'mongst men
    Being most unfit to live. I have made you mad;
    And even with such-like valour men hang and
        drown
    Their proper selves.

ALONSO, SEBASTIAN & c. draw their swords

You fools! I and my fellows
Are ministers of Fate: the elements,
Of whom your swords are temper'd, may as well
Wound the loud winds, or with bemock'd-at stabs
Kill the still-closing waters, as diminish
One dowle that's in my plume: my fellow-ministers
Are like invulnerable. If you could hurt,
Your swords are now too massy for your strengths
And will not be uplifted. But remember –
For that's my business to you – that you three
From Milan did supplant good Prospero;
Expos'd unto the sea, which hath requit it,
Him, and his innocent child: for which foul deed
The powers, delaying, not forgetting, have
Incens'd the seas and shores, yea, all the creatures,
Against your peace. Thee of thy son, Alonso,
They have bereft; and do pronounce by me:
Lingering perdition, worse than any death
Can be at once, shall step by step attend
You and your ways; whose wraths to guard you from –
Which here, in this most desolate isle, else falls
Upon your heads – is nothing but heart-sorrow
And a clear life ensuing.

He vanishes in thunder; then, to soft music enter the Shapes again, and dance, with mocks and mows, and carry out the table

William Shakespeare

TEXT LEVEL WORK

Comprehension

A 1 Who is Prospero?

2 What is the name of the port from which the nobles sailed?

3 What weapons do the shipwrecked nobles carry?

4 What is the name of the spirit who delivers warnings to the nobles?

5 Of which city was Prospero once the ruler?

B 1 Explain the following in your own words:

    a '*A kind of excellent dumb discourse.*'

    b '*... my fellow-ministers*
      Are like invulnerable.'

    c '*... too massy for your strengths*
      And will not be uplifted.'

2 What do you learn of the spirits of the island from the extract? Quote from the extract in support of your views.

3 What do you learn when Alonso says:

'Brother, my lord the duke,
Stand to and do as we.'

4 Using evidence from the text, show how Prospero renders the shipwrecked nobles defenceless.

C Using evidence from the text, what can you infer about the differences in the world of the shipwrecked nobles and the world of the island? You should comment on:

- the world in which the nobles would normally live
- the world which Prospero lives in, on the island
- Prospero's motives in bringing the nobles to the island
- the ways in which Shakespeare creates an extraordinary atmosphere on the island.

WORD LEVEL WORK

Vocabulary

Dictionary and contextual work
Use a dictionary and the context of the passage to explain the meaning of the following words:

1 banquet	5 viands	9 surfeited
2 drollery	6 dewlapp'd	10 bereft
3 phoenix	7 warrant	11 supplant
4 discourse	8 harpy	12 perdition

Spelling

'ounce' words
Key word: **ounce**

1 Use the key word in a sentence of your own.

2 Learn these important 'ounce' words:

ren**ounce**	fl**ounce**	p**ounce**
ann**ounce**	ann**ounce**ment	tr**ounce**

SENTENCE LEVEL WORK

Grammar and punctuation

Phrasal verbs

> Verbs are sometimes combined, in short phrases, with adverbs or prepositions, or both. These phrases sometimes carry subtle shades of meaning, or fine distinctions, that do not rely on the basic meanings of the words.
> **Phrasal verbs** are usually either **literal**, **semi-idiomatic** or **idiomatic**.

- **Literal**: the verb, the short adverb or preposition maintains a literal meaning, eg

  'take down the box'   'walk across the grass'
  'climb out of the boat'.

- **Semi-idiomatic**: the verb keeps its meaning, but the short adverb or preposition adds a nuance that is not obvious from its basic meaning. Though the exact meaning of these phrasal verbs may not be clear, the rough meaning can be guessed from language clues, eg

  'hand out'   'hand in'   'hand over'
  'drive on'   'drive up'   'drive off'.

- **Idiomatic**: these phrasal verbs are not predictable from the basic meanings of the verb, the short adverb or the preposition, eg

  'carry on'   'come across'   'put up with'   'live up to'.

Copy and complete the table. State whether the sentences are Literal (L), Semi-idiomatic (S) or Idiomatic (I).

Phrasal verbs	Type
Hang your jacket up.	
Dad can *count on* my help.	
I watched Max *sneak up on* Ellie.	
Alice tries to *fit in with* everybody.	
Michael *jumped up* on the hedgerow.	
It is hard to *bring up* children as a lone parent.	
The hotelier tried not to *bring up* the subject of the war.	
The old man *held onto* his wife for support.	
The children were told not to *run through* the kitchen.	
Chloe was asked to *get down off* the ladder.	

TEXT LEVEL WORK

Writing

The world of the play

When we watch a play, we enter into a contract where we agree to believe in a world created by the writer, acted out by the performers. This is sometimes called 'suspending disbelief'. From the first scene, the characters and actions create a world, set in time and place. However, this world is only the first of two worlds that the writer creates to tell their story.

Language features
The ordinary world
The first world is a point of reference, sometimes called the *ordinary world*.

This is the world where the main character, the *protagonist* of the play, lives. In *The Tempest*, the ordinary world is the island on which Prospero was cast away. The playwright establishes this world clearly at the beginning, then the protagonist chooses to take action to leave the ordinary world for another world, the world of the story that is to be told.

The call to action

When the protagonist makes a choice to act that will cause him or her to leave the ordinary world and enter the world of the story, it is known as the *call to action*. The world of the story that is to unfold is called the *extraordinary world*.

In *The Tempest*, the decision to cause the ship to be wrecked and the nobles to be washed up on the island is Prospero's call to action.

Prospero's ordinary world is going to be transformed into the extraordinary world in which the shipwrecked nobles find themselves. The world of the story becomes the world of the shipwrecked nobles with their new and unusual companions, Prospero's spirit servants.

The extraordinary world

Entering the extraordinary world is the result of action taken by the protagonist. The extraordinary world is the world of the unfolding story. The beginning of a play ends when the protagonist has moved into this new world. The second stage in the development of the play contains most of the conflict and is firmly rooted in the extraordinary world of the story. The final stage in a play is when the call to action reaches its climax and the actions are resolved.

Defining the two worlds

The writing assignment will have more focus if you define clearly and simply:

- the ordinary world where the protagonist lives day-to-day, the starting point of the hero's journey
- the call to action in which the protagonist responds to events by doing something, making a choice and performing an action, that will propel him toward the world of the story
- the extraordinary world of the story itself, where the hero is challenged and tested, and where he or she will win, usually, and become wiser for the struggle.

Writing assignment

Write a play scene in which a protagonist, based in an ordinary world, decides to act and the story moves into an extraordinary world. Use the information in the language features to help you check that you have established:

- setting
- character of the protagonist
- reason for taking action
- the extraordinary world in which the protagonist meets other characters.

You do not need to tell the whole story. Just take the story into the extraordinary world and break off at an appropriate moment, as the extract from *The Tempest* does.

Personal choice

Choose one of the following assignments.

1 Write a play scene which uses the idea of beginning in an ordinary world, with a protagonist making a choice to act, then carry out a transition into the extraordinary world of the developing story.

2 Watch a film version, or a live performance of *The Tempest*. Write a critical evaluation of the production you have seen.

my good comfort.

In A Winter's Tale, Shakespeare tells the story of Leontes, King of Sicily, who thinks his wife, Hermione, is dead. He is presented with a 'statue' in the chapel at Paulina's house (a fearless noblewoman loyal to the queen), which is really his wife pretending.

Act V, Scene 3

LEONTES

As now she might have done,
So much to my good comfort, as it is
Now piercing to my soul. O, thus she stood,
Even with such life of majesty, warm life,
As now it coldly stands, when first I woo'd her!
I am ashamed: does not the stone rebuke me
For being more stone than it? O royal piece,
There's magic in thy majesty, which has
My evils conjured to remembrance and
From thy admiring daughter took the spirits,
Standing like stone with thee.

PERDITA

And give me leave,
And do not say 'tis superstition, that
I kneel and then implore her blessing. Lady,
Dear queen, that ended when I but began,
Give me that hand of yours to kiss.

PAULINA

O, patience!
The statue is but newly fix'd, the colour's not dry.

CAMILLO

My lord, your sorrow was too sore laid on,
Which sixteen winters cannot blow away,
So many summers dry; scarce any joy
Did ever so long live; no sorrow
But kill'd itself much sooner.

POLIXENES

Dear my brother,
Let him that was the cause of this have power
To take off so much grief from you as he
Will piece up in himself.

PAULINA

Indeed, my lord,
If I had thought the sight of my poor image
Would thus have wrought you, –
    for the stone is mine –
I'd not have show'd it.

LEONTES

Do not draw the curtain.

PAULINA

No longer shall you gaze on't, lest your fancy
May think anon it moves.

LEONTES

Let be, let be.
Would I were dead, but that, methinks, already –
What was he that did make it? See, my lord,

Would you not deem it breathed? and that those veins
Did verily bear blood?

POLIXENES

Masterly done:
The very life seems warm upon her lip.

LEONTES

The fixture of her eye has motion in't,
As we are mock'd with art.

PAULINA

I'll draw the curtain:
My lord's almost so far transported that
He'll think anon it lives.

LEONTES

O sweet Paulina,
Make me to think so twenty years together!
No settled senses of the world can match
The pleasure of that madness. Let 't alone.

PAULINA

I am sorry, sir, I have thus far stirr'd you: but
I could afflict you farther.

LEONTES

Do, Paulina;
For this affliction has a taste as sweet
As any cordial comfort. Still, methinks,
There is an air comes from her: what fine chisel
Could ever yet cut breath? Let no man mock me,
For I will kiss her.

PAULINA

Good my lord, forbear:
The ruddiness upon her lip is wet;
You'll mar it if you kiss it, stain your own
With oily painting. Shall I draw the curtain?

LEONTES

No, not these twenty years.

PERDITA

So long could I
Stand by, a looker on.

PAULINA

Either forbear,
Quit presently the chapel, or resolve you
For more amazement. If you can behold it,
I'll make the statue move indeed, descend
And take you by the hand; but then you'll think –
Which I protest against – I am assisted
By wicked powers.

LEONTES

What you can make her do,

I am content to look on: what to speak,
I am content to hear; for 'tis as easy
To make her speak as move.

PAULINA
It is required
You do awake your faith. Then all stand
    still;
On: those that think it is unlawful
    business
I am about, let them depart.

LEONTES
Proceed:
No foot shall stir.

PAULINA
Music, awake her; strike!

Music
'Tis time; descend; be stone no more;
    approach;
Strike all that look upon with marvel.
    Come,

I'll fill your grave up: stir, nay, come
    away,
Bequeath to death your numbness,
    for from him
Dear life redeems you. You perceive
    she stirs:

HERMIONE comes down
Start not; her actions shall be holy as
You hear my spell is lawful: do not
    shun her
Until you see her die again; for then
You kill her double. Nay, present your
    hand:
When she was young you woo'd her;
    now in age
Is she become the suitor?

LEONTES
O, she's warm!
If this be magic, let it be an art
Lawful as eating.

William Shakespeare

TEXT LEVEL WORK

Comprehension

A 1 Who is pretending to be a statue?

2 What is the name of the king who thinks his wife is dead?

3 What is the name of the lady who is stage-managing the presentation of the statue to the king?

4 What is the signal for the statue to come to life?

5 Where does the presentation of the statue to the king take place?

B 1 Explain the following in your own words:

a '*I am ashamed: does not the stone rebuke me
For being more stone than it?*'

b '*There's magic in thy majesty, which has
My evils conjured to remembrance and
From thy admiring daughter took the spirits ...*'

c '*The fixture of her eye has motion in't,
As we are mock'd with art.*'

2 What is the relationship between Perdita and the woman of the statue? Quote from the extract in support of your views.

3 What do you learn when Camillo says:
'*My lord, your sorrow was too sore laid on,
Which sixteen winters cannot blow away ...*'
What does this tell us about Perdita?

4 Why does Paulina say:

'*... then you'll think –*
Which I protest against – I am assisted
By wicked powers.'?

What are the others likely to think about the statue coming to life?

C Using evidence from the text, what can you infer about the features that make the statue seem alive? You should comment on:

- physical details
- remarks made by the characters
- the emotional impact on Leontes and his companions.

WORD LEVEL WORK

Vocabulary

Dictionary and contextual work

Use a dictionary and the context of the passage to explain the meaning of the following words:

1 conjured	4 deem	7 transported	10 forbear
2 superstition	5 verily	8 affliction	11 bequeath
3 fancy	6 Masterly	9 cordial	12 redeems

Spelling

'sure' words

Key word: plea**sure**

1 Use the key word in a sentence of your own.

2 Learn these important 'sure' words:

   mea**sure**   lei**sure**   pres**sure**

SENTENCE LEVEL WORK

Grammar and punctuation

Sentence fluency

Sentence fluency is the way the language flows, using rhythm and the patterns of word sounds. The way in which the writing sounds pleasant to the ear is carefully crafted in its construction. Writers achieve good sentence fluency through:

- creative phrasing, eg

   '*... this affliction has a taste*
   as sweet
   As any cordial comfort.'

- repetition, eg

   '***I am content*** *to look on:*
   what to speak,
   I am content *to hear ...*'

- alliteration and assonance, eg

   '*...* **s***pirits,*
   Standing like **s***tone ...*'

- variety in sentence length, eg

   '*O, patience!*'

Copy and complete the table. State whether the examples are creative phrasing (CP), repetition (R), alliteration/assonance (A), or variation in sentence length (VSL).

Examples	Type
Bequeath to death your numbness	
this affliction has a taste as sweet	
does not the stone rebuke me For being more stone than it?	
magic in thy majesty	
You do awake your faith. Then all stand still; On: those that think it is unlawful business I am about, let them depart.	
what fine chisel	
Could ever yet cut breath? Indeed, my lord, If I had thought the sight of my poor image Would thus have wrought you, – for the stone is mine – I'd not have show'd it.	
I am content to look on: what to speak, I am content to hear; for 'tis as easy To make her speak as move.	

TEXT LEVEL WORK

Writing

Sentence fluency

> Sentence fluency means the ways in which the writer manipulates the rhythm and flow of the language. They may use the patterns of the sounds of words, to play to the ear, as well as the eye.
>
> In *A Winter's Tale*, Shakespeare achieves a high level of fluency through creative phrasing, alliteration, rhyme and variety in sentence length and structure.

Language features

Rhythm and meter

- an easy flow and sense of rhythm, eg
  '*What you can make her do,*
  I am content to look on: what to speak,
  I am content to hear ...'

- cadence – emphasise the sound of the words as well as meaning, eg
  '*Dear queen, that ended when I but began*'.

Rhyme and alliteration

- rhyme, rhythm, meter, alliteration and repetition are used for effect, eg
  '*... the spirits,*
  Standing like stone with thee.'

- Dialogue sounds natural, within its context, eg

   'I'll make the statue move indeed, descend
   And take you by the hand ...'.

Variety in sentence structure

- purposeful and varied sentence beginnings add variety and energy, eg

   'O, she's warm!
   If this be magic, let it be an art
   Lawful as eating.'

- sentences are well built, with strong and varied structures, eg

   'It is required
   You do awake your faith. Then all stand still;
   On: those that think it is unlawful business
   I am about, let them depart.'

- sentences reinforce the meaning. Creative and appropriate connectives between sentences shows how they relate to and build upon the ones that came before and after, eg

   'PAULINA
   Good my lord, forbear: ...
   With oily painting. Shall I draw the curtain?
   LEONTES
   No, not these twenty years.
   PERDITA
   So long could I
   Stand by, a looker on.'

Variety in sentence length

- sentences vary in length as well as structure, eg

   'Let be, let be.
   Would I were dead, but that, methinks, already –
   What was he that did make it?'

- sentence fragments are used deliberately to add style, rather than accidentally, eg
   'O, patience!'

Writing assignment

Imagine a character who has been tricked into believing in an illusion, eg Leontes believing that his wife was dead. Write a play scene in which a protagonist is manipulated into responding with great emotion to a representation, eg the statue in *A Winter's Tale*. Finish the scene when the illusion is reversed and the protagonist realises that they have been tricked. Make sure that you reveal the emotions of the protagonist, after the illusion has been reversed. Use the information in the language features to help you check that you have manipulated the sentence fluency effectively:

- rhythm and metre
- rhyme and alliteration
- sentence structure
- sentence length.

Personal choice

Choose one of the following assignments.

1 Write a play scene about a person being tricked. Vary the sentence lengths and rhythms of the dialogue to change the mood, eg from tension to happiness.

2 Watch a live performance, or a filmed version of *A Winter's Tale*. Write a critical evaluation of the production you have seen.

One face,
one voice

In Twelfth Night, twins Sebastian and Viola have been shipwrecked and separated, in a hostile country. Viola disguises herself as a boy, Cesario, but is caught up in a romantic tangle with Duke Orsino and the Lady Olivia. Duke Orsino loves Olivia; Olivia loves Cesario (Viola); Cesario loves Duke Orsino. Sebastian loves Olivia, who thinks he is Cesario. Sebastian is befriended and given money by Antonio, an enemy of the duke. Antonio mistakenly thinks he has been betrayed when Cesario (Sebastian's twin) denies any knowledge of his friendship, or the money. As friends, rivals and lovers mistake Cesario for Sebastian, and Sebastian for Cesario, the reality and the illusion is revealed.

Act V, Scene 1

DUKE ORSINO
    One face, one voice, one habit, and two persons –
    A natural perspective, that is and is not!
SEBASTIAN
    Antonio! O my dear Antonio!
    How have the hours rack'd and tortured me,
    Since I have lost thee!
ANTONIO
    Sebastian are you?
SEBASTIAN
    Fear'st thou that, Antonio?
ANTONIO
    How have you made division of yourself?
    An apple, cleft in two, is not more twin
    Than these two creatures. Which is Sebastian?
OLIVIA
    Most wonderful!
SEBASTIAN
    Do I stand there? I never had a brother;
    Nor can there be that deity in my nature
    Of here and everywhere. I had a sister,
    Whom the blind waves and surges have devourèd.
    Of charity, what kin are you to me?
    What countryman? what name? what parentage?
VIOLA
    Of Messaline: Sebastian was my father;
    Such a Sebastian was my brother too,
    So went he suited to his wat'ry tomb.
    If spirits can assume both form and suit,
    You come to fright us.
SEBASTIAN
    A spirit I am indeed,
    But am in that dimension grossly clad
    Which from the womb I did participate.

    Were you a woman – as the rest goes even –
    I should my tears let fall upon your cheek,
    And say 'Thrice-welcome, drownèd Viola!'
VIOLA
    My father had a mole upon his brow.
SEBASTIAN
    And so had mine.
VIOLA
    And died that day when Viola from her birth
    Had numbered thirteen years.
SEBASTIAN
    O, that record is lively in my soul!
    He finishèd indeed his mortal act
    That day that made my sister thirteen years.
VIOLA
    If nothing lets to make us happy both,
    But this my masculine usurped attire,
    Do not embrace me till each circumstance
    Of place, time, fortune, do cohere and jump
    That I am Viola: which to confirm,
    I'll bring you to a captain in this town,
    Where lie my maiden weeds; by whose gentle help
    I was preserved – to serve this noble count.
    All the occurrence of my fortune since
    Hath been between this lady and this lord.
SEBASTIAN [*To OLIVIA*]
    So comes it, lady, you have been mistook.
    But nature to her bias drew in that.
    You would have been contracted to a maid;
    Nor are you therein, by my life, deceived,
    You are betrothed both to a maid and man.

William Shakespeare

TEXT LEVEL WORK

Comprehension

A 1 Who are the twins in the extract?

2 What is the name of the Duke?

3 Who is Cesario?

4 What was the name of Viola's father?

5 Where do Viola and Sebastian come from?

B 1 Explain the following in your own words:

a '*One face, one voice, one habit, and two persons ...*'

b '*I'll bring you to a captain in this town,*
   Where lie my maiden weeds ...'

c '*He finishèd indeed his mortal act*
   That day that made my sister thirteen years.'

2 What is the relationship between Olivia and Sebastian? Quote from the extract in support of your views.

3 What do you learn when Sebastian says:
   '*You would have been contracted to a maid;*
   Nor are you therein, by my life, deceived,
   You are betrothed both to a maid and man'?

4 Why does Sebastian say:
   '*A spirit I am indeed,*
   But am in that dimension grossly clad
   Which from the womb I did participate'?

C Using evidence from the text, what can you infer about how Shakespeare confuses reality and illusion in the play? You should comment on:

- physical details
- remarks made by the characters
- the emotional impact of the revelations on the characters
- how the language emphasises the confusions caused by the twins.

WORD LEVEL WORK

Vocabulary

Dictionary and contextual work
Use a dictionary and the context of the passage to explain the meaning of the following words:

1 perspective	5 devoured	9 attire
2 cleft	6 dimension	10 cohere
3 deity	7 grossly	11 weeds
4 surges	8 usurped	12 betrothed

Spelling

'age' words
Key word: parent**age**

1 Use the key word in a sentence of your own.

2 Learn these important 'age' words:

age   aver**age**   pilgrim**age**   s**age**

SENTENCE LEVEL WORK

Grammar and punctuation

Language changes over time

One of the amazing things about words is that they all have a history, some English words going back thousands of years. Words such as 'one', 'two' and other low numbers, or words like 'father', 'mother' and other basic family words, have been used for thousands of years without changing their meaning. Other words are very recent, eg the word 'smog' (a blend of 'smoke' and 'fog') or 'radar' (an acronym based on the phrase 'radio detecting and ranging').

Studying the history of a word, from its beginnings through to the present time, in a methodical way, is called **etymology**. Etymology explores how a word is pronounced and how it has developed over time, eg the word 'ship' used to be pronounced as if it were 'skip'. Etymology also examines how grammar has changed, eg the modern verb 'to network' did not exist as a verb 50 years ago. A word's meaning is also explained, eg 'the web' had a different meaning ten years ago.

The ways in which words change varies. Words often change in meaning independently of one another. Words are modified in unpredictable ways over time. Changes in pronunciation are the most regular, eg the word 'show' was once pronounced with a 'k', just like 'ship'. Changes in the grammar of a word are less predictable.

Copy and complete the table by using an etymological dictionary to find the meanings of the expressions. Write a sentence for each, suggesting explanations of how these expressions came into use. The first one has been done for you.

Expression	Etymological explanation
fiasco	used in old Italian expression, *far fiasco*, ie *to make a bottle*. Italian for *bottle* or *flask*. Came to be associated with breakages or failures.
bead	
to use one's head	
foot of the hill	
mouth of a river	
mouth off	
knee-jerk reaction	
to ship a package	
to park a car	

TEXT LEVEL WORK

Writing

Standard and non-standard language

People tend to think that older forms of language are more elegant and correct than modern usage. By 'correct English', people really mean standard English. Languages have a standard form used by government, education and other formal users. Standard English is just one dialect of English and every dialect has language rules of its own.

Language is always changing and adapting to the needs of the people who use it. Language changes for a number of reasons:

- everyone has different language experiences, learning different language forms, depending on region, age, education or occupation
- new experiences, products and technology need new words to describe them
- groups use language to reinforce their group identity
- words are borrowed from other languages as travel increases
- proper names become associated with a particular appliance or use, eg vacuum cleaners are often referred to as 'Hoovers'
- new words are created by mistaken use of an existing word, eg 400 years ago, either a single pea, or many, was described by the word 'pease'. Gradually, people assumed that 'pease' was the plural, and 'pea' must be the singular.

Shakespeare's language was different enough from modern English to make it difficult for young people to understand easily. His language differs in a variety of ways.

Language features

Words change over time
For example:

- 'An apple, cleft in two' – Shakespearean
- 'An apple, cut in half' – modern.

Changes in word order
For example:

- 'A natural perspective, that is and is not!' – Shakespearean
- 'That is and is not a natural perspective!' – modern.

Reversal of subject and verb
For example:

- 'So went he suited to his watery tomb' – Shakespearean
- 'So suited he went to his watery tomb' – modern.

Omitting the (understood) subject of a verb
For example:

- 'But am in that dimension grossly clad' – Shakespearean
- 'But I am grossly clad in that dimension' – modern.

Changes in regularity or irregularity of verb forms
For example:

- 'lady, you have been mistook' – Shakespearean
- 'lady, you have been mistaken' – modern.

Patterns of repetition
These give emphasis to a point being made, eg

- 'One face, one voice, one habit, and two persons'.

Apostrophe, or exclamation
In Shakespearean times, these were used to add dramatic stress to dialogue, eg

- 'O my dear Antonio**!**'

Idiomatic expressions arise and disappear
For example:

- '**Of charity**, what kin are you to me?'

Pronunciation of the verb endings, and the punctuation that may be used to show it
For example:

- 'You are betrothed both to a maid and man.
  "Thrice-welcome, drown**è**d Viola!"'

Formal and informal forms of 'you', 'thee' and 'thou'
For example:

- 'ANTONIO   Sebastian are **you**?
  SEBASTIAN   Fear'st **thou** that, Antonio?'

Writing assignment
Write a translation of the extract from *Twelfth Night*, transcribing it into either formal, standard, modern English *or* an informal dialect of modern English. Then, using the language features to help you, write an explanation of how your language differs from Shakespeare's. You should consider:

- words change over time
- changes in word order
- reversal of subject and verb
- omitting the (understood) subject of a verb
- changes in regularity or irregularity of verb forms
- patterns of repetition give emphasis to a point being made
- apostrophe or exclamation is used to add dramatic stress to dialogue
- idiomatic expressions that arise and disappear
- pronunciation of the verb endings
- use of formal and informal forms of 'you', 'thee' and 'thou'.

Personal choice

Choose one of the following assignments.

1 Imagine that you have been transported back in time to the Shakespearean period. Write an explanation for Shakespeare about how language has changed since his time, giving examples.

2 Write a play scene, based on the confusions caused by twins. Experiment with writing the scene in Shakespearean style language.

I've no kit, Sir.

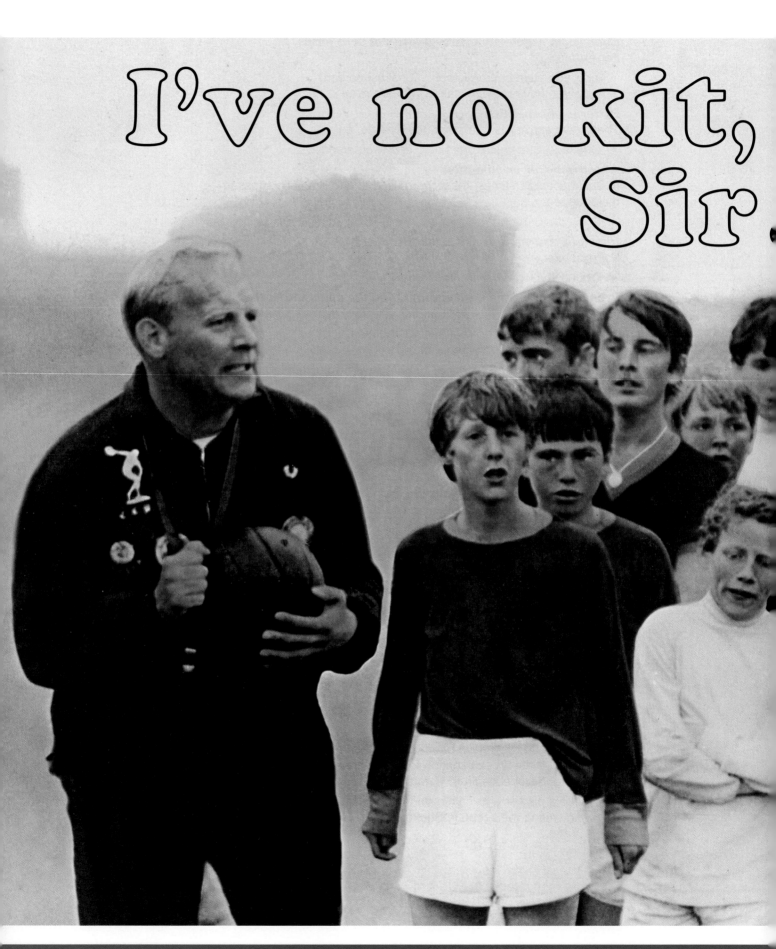

He walked into the changing room as clean and shining as a boy down for breakfast on his seaside holidays. The other boys were packed into the aisles between the rows of pegs, their hanging clothes partitioning the room into corridors. Mr Sugden was passing slowly across one end of the room, looking down the corridors and counting the boys as they changed. He was wearing a violet tracksuit. The top was embellished with cloth badges depicting numerous crests and qualifications, and on the breast a white athlete carried the Olympic torch. The legs were tucked into new white football socks, neatly folded at his ankles, and his football boots were polished as black and shiny as the bombs used by assassins in comic strips. The laces binding them had been scrubbed white, and both boots had been fastened identically: two loops of the foot and one of the ankle, and tied in a neat bow under the tab at the back.

He finished counting and rolled a football off the window sill into his hand. The leather was rich with dubbin, and the new orange lace nipped the slit as firmly as a row of surgical stitches. He tossed it up and caught it on the ends of his fingers, then turned round to Billy.

'Skyving again, Casper?'

'No, Sir, Mr Farthing wanted me; he's been talking to me.'

'I bet that was stimulating for him, wasn't it?'

'What does that mean, Sir?'

'The conversation, lad, what do you think it means?'

'No, Sir, that word, stimult ... stimult-ting.'

'Stimulating you fool, S-T-I-M-U-L-A-T-I-N-G, stimulating!'

'Yes, Sir.'

'Well get changed lad, you're two weeks late already!'

He lifted the elastic webbing of one cuff and rotated his fist to look at his watch on the underside of his wrist.

'Some of us want a game even if you don't.'

'I've no kit, Sir.'

Mr Sugden stepped back and slowly looked Billy up and down, his top lip curling.

'Casper, you make me SICK.'

'SICK' penetrated the hubbub, which immediately decreased as the boys stopped their own conversations and turned their attention to Mr Sugden and Billy.

'Every lesson it's the same old story. "Please, Sir, I've no kit".'

The boys tittered at his whipped-dog whining impersonation.

'Every lesson for four years! And in all that time you've made no attempt whatsoever to get any kit, you've skyved and scrounged and borrowed and ...'

He tried this lot on one breath, and his ruddy complexion heightened and glowed like a red balloon as he held his breath and fought for another verb.

'...and ... BEG ...' The balloon burst and the pronunciation of the verb disintegrated.

'Why is it that everyone else can get some but you can't?'

'I don't know, Sir. My mother won't buy me any. She says it's a waste of money, especially now that I'm leaving.'

'You haven't been leaving for four years, have you?'

'No, Sir.'

'You could have bought some out of your spending money, couldn't you?'

'I don't like football, Sir.'

'What's that got to do with it?'

'I don't know, Sir. Anyway I don't get enough.'

'Get a job then, I don't ...'

'I've got one, Sir.'

'Well then! You get paid, don't you?'

'Yes, Sir. But I have to gi' it to my mam. I'm still payin' her for my fines, like instalments every week.'

Mr Sugden bounced the ball on Billy's head, compressing his neck into his shoulders.

'Well, you should keep out of trouble then, lad, and then ...'

'I haven't been in trouble, Sir, not ...'

'Shut up, lad! Shut up, before you drive me crackers!'

He hit Billy twice with the ball, holding it between both hands as though murdering him with a boulder. The rest of the class grinned behind each other's backs, or placed their fingers over their mouths to suppress the laughter gathering there. They watched Mr Sugden rush into his changing room, and began to giggle, stopping immediately he reappeared waving a pair of giant blue drawers.

'Here Casper, get them on!'

He wanged them across the room, and Billy caught them flying over his head, and held them up for inspection as though he was contemplating buying. The class roared. They would have made Billy two suits and an overcoat.

'They'll not fit me, Sir.'

The class roared again and even Billy had to smile. There was only Mr Sugden not amused.

'What are you talking about, lad? You can get them on, can't you?'

'Yes, Sir.'

'Well they fit you then! Now get changed, QUICK.'

Billy found an empty peg and hung his jacket on it. He was immediately enclosed in a tight square as two lines of boys formed up, one on each side of him between the parallel curtains of clothing. He sat down on the long bench covering the shoe racks, and worked his jeans over his pumps. Mr Sugden broke one side of the square and stood over him.

'And you want your underpants and vest off.'

'I don't wear 'em, Sir.'

As he reached up to hang his trousers on the peg, his shirt lap lifted, revealing his bare cheeks, which looked as smooth and boney as two white billiard balls. He stepped into the shorts and pulled them up to his waist. The legs reached halfway down his shins. He pulled the waist up to his neck and his knees just slid into view. Boys pointed at them, shouting and laughing into each other's faces, and other boys who were still changing rushed to the scene, jumping up on the benches or parting the curtains to see through. And at the centre of it all, Billy, like a brave little clown, was busy trying to make them fit, and Sugden was looking at him as though it was his fault for being too small for them.

'Roll them down and don't be so foolish. You're too daft to laugh at, Casper.'

Barry Hines

TEXT LEVEL WORK

Comprehension

A 1 Why is Billy late for the PE lesson?

2 Why doesn't Billy get changed for the lesson?

3 What is Billy's excuse?

4 Why can't he buy his own kit?

5 How does Mr Sugden solve the problem?

B 1 Explain in your own words the effect the writer intends by the use of these similes:

    a '*... his ruddy complexion heightened and glowed like a red balloon ...*'
    b '*... as smooth and boney as two white billiard balls.*'
    c '*... like a brave little clown ...*'.

2 Why do you think the writer has the other boys laughing and enjoying the scene between Billy and Mr Sugden?

3 What do you think Mr Sugden's motives are when he makes Billy put on the oversized pair of shorts?

4 At the end of the extract, who do you think 'comes out on top'?

C What impression does the writer give of Mr Sugden's character? Support your view with evidence from the text. You should consider:

- his personal appearance
- the way he talks to Billy
- what he does to Billy.

WORD LEVEL WORK

Vocabulary

Dictionary and contextual work
Use a dictionary and the context of the extract to explain the meaning of the following words:

1 partitioning	5 stimulating	9 instalments
2 embellished	6 penetrated	10 compressing
3 depicting	7 hubbub	11 wanged
4 dubbin	8 disintegrated	12 contemplating

Spelling

'ate' words
Key words: rot**ate**   stimul**ate**   penetr**ate**   contempl**ate**

  1 Use these key words in sentences of your own.

  2 Learn these important 'ate' words:

      chocol**ate**   separ**ate**   clim**ate**   estim**ate**

SENTENCE LEVEL WORK

Grammar and punctuation

Adjectival clauses

Remember. A **complex sentence** is made up of an **independent clause**, which can make sense by itself, and a **dependent clause**. There are three kinds of dependent clauses:

- adjectival clauses
- adverbial clauses
- noun clauses.

The adjectival clause gives extra information about a noun or a pronoun. It will begin with a relative pronoun ('who', 'whose', 'whom', 'which' and 'that') or a subordinate conjunction ('when' and 'where'). The subject is often separated from its verb by the dependent clause, eg:

Mr Sugden, who was frustrated by Billy, hit him on the head with the ball.

subject   adjective clauses   dependent adjectival clause   verb

Copy the sentences below and underline, colour or highlight the adjectival clauses.

1 Mr Sugden, who was always neatly turned out, wore a violet tracksuit.

2 Billy Casper, whose school career was a disaster, had no football kit.

3 From the other boys, who were contemptuous, Billy received no sympathy.

4 Billy, when faced with PE, always found excuses not to take part.

5 In the changing rooms, Billy, who never had any kit, was humiliated by Mr Sugden.

6 The other boys laughed at Billy's humiliation, while he was changing.

TEXT LEVEL WORK

Writing

Changing the time and the viewpoint

This extract from *Kes* is written in the third person which means that the narrator is not one of the characters involved. The reader sees the episode and understands the characters through:

- the narrative
- the dialogue
- as it is happening.

Language features

Narrative

The parts of a story where the third person narrator is 'speaking' to the reader is called the narrative. Writers can use narrative to:

- describe the physical appearance of the setting
- describe the physical appearance of the characters
- explain the thoughts and feelings of the characters
- move the plot along.

Dialogue

This part of the story is where the characters themselves speak and through their words the reader:

- gets to know them
- sees how they react in different situations
- assesses their relationships with other characters.

Writing assignment

Some stories are written in the first person as if one of the characters is telling the story. Some stories have more than one narrator so the reader sees the same incidents from two different viewpoints. This is called multiple narration.

Write the incident in the PE changing room from Billy's point of view, followed immediately from Mr Sugden's point of view. Each is looking back on the incident and, while their account of *what* happens should be fairly similar, their attitude to their own behaviour and that of the other character will be very different.

Personal choice

Choose one of the following assignments.

1 Imagine that Billy refused to put on the shorts. Write an alternative ending for the incident using both narration and dialogue.

2 Write a paragraph to explain why you would, or would not, like to read the rest of the story.

I'm not you

Confessions of a Born Spectator

One infant grows up and becomes a jockey,
Another plays basketball or hockey,
This one the prize ring hastes to enter,
That one becomes a tackle or centre.
I'm just as glad as glad can be
That I'm not them, that they're not me.

With all my heart do I admire
Athletes who sweat for fun or hire,
Who take the field in gaudy pomp
And maim each other as they romp;
My limp and bashful spirit feeds
On other people's heroic deeds.

Now A runs ninety yards to score;
B knocks the champion to the floor;
C risking vertebrae and spine,
Lashes his steed across the line.
You'd think my ego it would please
To swap positions with one of these.

Well, ego might be pleased enough,
But zealous athletes play so rough;
They do not ever, in their dealings,
Consider one another's feelings.
I'm glad that when my struggle begins
Twixt prudence and ego, prudence wins.

When swollen eye meets gnarled fist,
When snaps the knee, and cracks the wrist,
When calm officialdom demands,
Is there a doctor in the stands?
My soul in true thanksgiving speaks
For this most modest of physiques.

Athletes, I'll drink to you or eat with you,
Or anything except compete with you;
Buy tickets worth their weight in radium
To watch you gambol in a stadium,
And reassure myself anew
That you're not me and I'm not you.

Ogden Nash

Skiing

Skiing is like being
part of a mountain.
On the early morning run
before the crowds begin,
my skis make
   little blizzards
as they plough
   through untouched powder
to leave fresh tracks
   in the blue-white snow.
My body bends and turns
   to catch each
bend and turn
   the mountain takes;
and I am the mountain
and the mountain is me.

Bobbi Katz

Extract from

There's a Breathless Hush
in the Close Tonight

There's a breathless hush in the Close tonight –
Ten to make and a match to win –
A bumping pitch and a blinding light,
An hour to play and the last man in.
And it's not for the sake of the ribboned coat,
Or the selfish hope of a season's fame,
But his Captain's hand on his shoulder smote –
'Play up! Play up! and play the game!'

Sir Henry Newbolt

TEXT LEVEL WORK

Comprehension

A 1 In which of the poems does the poet like to take part in an individual sport?

2 In which poem is the sportsman part of a team?

3 Which poet has no wish to be a sportsman?

4 In verse three of *Confessions of a Born Spectator*, what three sports is the poet referring to?

5 Which sport is written about in *There's a Breathless Hush in the Close Tonight*?

B 1 In your own words, sum up Ogden Nash's attitude to sport and his reasons.

2 In contrast to Nash, what aspect of the sport does Katz not consider in his poem?

3 Explain in your own words:

'And it's not for the sake of the ribboned coat.
Or the selfish hope of a season's fame ...'.

4 Explain which of the poems appeals most to you and why.

C Compare and contrast the poems *Skiing* and *There's a Breathless Hush in the Close Tonight*. You should consider:

- the nature of the sport
- the reason why the poet likes that particular sport
- the structure of each poem.

WORD LEVEL WORK

Vocabulary

Dictionary and contextual work
Use a dictionary and the context of the extract to explain the meaning of the following words:

Confessions of a Born Spectator

1 hastes
2 gaudy
3 maim
4 bashful
5 steed
6 ego
7 zealous
8 prudence
9 physiques
10 radium

There's a Breathless Hush in the Close Tonight

11 breathless
12 smote

Spelling

Words ending in 'o'
Key word: eg**o**

1 Use this key word in a sentence of your own.

2 Learn these important 'o' words:

portfoli**o**   rati**o**   ostinat**o**   temp**o**   impast**o**

> *HINT*
>
> *Many words ending in 'o' are borrowed from other languages.*

SENTENCE LEVEL WORK

Grammar and punctuation

Sentence construction – clause conjunctions

> Remember. Sentences may contain more than one **clause**. Clauses are joined together by **conjunctions**.
>
> - There must be a relationship of meaning between the clauses.
> - The conjunction used to join the clauses must be suitable for the relationship of meaning between the clauses.
>
> Clauses may:
>
> - be related by the idea of time, using conjunctions, eg 'before', 'after', 'during', 'since', 'while', 'when'
> - add an idea to another clause, joined using conjunctions, eg 'and', 'in addition', 'also', 'plus', 'furthermore', 'moreover'.
>
> Conjunctions may:
>
> - indicate that one clause is used to emphasise the other clause, eg 'indeed', 'in fact'
> - show that the two clauses demonstrate differences and should suggest the negative – think of it as 'not', eg 'however', 'nevertheless', 'but', 'although', 'yet'
> - come either at the beginning of a sentence, or in the middle of a sentence.
>
> Where the action of one clause only happens because of the other clause, this is called **condition** and the conjunction used is 'if'.
>
> Where one clause may cause another, this is called **causality**. The conjunctions needed include 'because', 'consequently', 'for', 'since', 'therefore'.

Copy and complete the table. Circle the conjunctions that are used to join the clauses. Write what type of relationship exists between the clauses: time, addition, emphasis, not, condition or causality.

Sentence	Relationship
Since we are all different, some people enjoy sport more than others.	
Ogden Nash also has good reasons for not liking sport.	
If you consider the physical injuries, you won't want to play rugby.	
Many sports attract participants and spectators, because they involve such high levels of skill.	
Most 'contact' sports involve some degree of physical danger; indeed, it is often this that attracts people who enjoy a challenge.	
Some sports attract those who enjoy team games, whereas other sports attract those who prefer individual activities.	

TEXT LEVEL WORK

Writing

Themes and styles

> The three poems, *Confessions of a Born Spectator*, *Skiing* and *There's a Breathless Hush in the Close Tonight*, share the common theme of sport but treat it in very different ways.

Language features

Structure and rhythm

Each poet has chosen a different verse structure for his poem:

- Ogden Nash has written in six regular verses with a regular rhythm which helps the poem to 'skip along', reflecting the humorous aspect of his musings about sport
- Bobbi Katz's poem is in one verse which snakes down the page reflecting the ski marks in the snow – a sophisticated shape poem
- the extract from a longer poem shows that Sir Henry Newbolt has concentrated on a strong, repetitive rhythm which reflects the tension building towards the climax of the cricket match.

Rhyme

In a similar way to structure and rhythm, each poet has made a conscious decision in the use of rhyme:

- Nash's poem uses rhyming couplets, three to a verse, eg
  > '*I'm just as glad as glad can **be***
  > *That I'm not them, and they're not **me**.*'
- Newbolt has used an ABAB rhyme scheme, eg
  > '*There's a breathless hush in the Close **tonight** –*
  > *Ten to make and a match to <u>win</u> –*
  > *A bumping pitch and a blinding **light**,*
  > *An hour to play and the last man <u>in</u>.*'
- Katz's poem does not rhyme so as not to interrupt the flowing motion of the words.

Writing assignment

Choose a particular sport that you are familiar with and write a poem in the style of either *Confessions of a Born Spectator*, *Skiing*, or *There's a Breathless Hush in the Close Tonight*. Your poem must leave the reader in no doubt as to your attitude to the sport.

Personal choice

Choose one of the following assignments.

1 If you modelled your poem on *Skiing*, use the same idea and write it in the style of either *Confessions of a Born Spectator* or *There's a Breathless Hush in the Close Tonight*, which means attention to structure, rhythm and rhyme.

2 If you modelled your poem on *Confessions of a Born Spectator* or *There's a Breathless Hush in the Close Tonight*, use the same idea and write it in the style of *Skiing*, which means the shape of the poem on the page reflects the sport in question and the poem does not rhyme.

Give us the ball

Scene 5 The football trial.
(Six boys appear. They are the aspiring strikers. They are keen but lack style. They are not natural footballers.)

BOY 1   Give us the ball will you.
BOY 2   These bloody boots are too small.
BOY 3   I must be mad.
BOY 1   I said give us the ball.
BOY 3   Why do I want to play for the worst team in the history of schoolboy football?
BOY 2   I think I've tied them up too tight.
BOY 1   For Godsake give us a touch.
BOY 4   (*He has the ball.*) This ball's too heavy.

(PHIL comes up to the group. He has a clipboard and a stop watch. He is disappointed at the turn-out.)

PHIL   Where's the rest then?
BOYS   Rest, sir?
PHIL   Is this all there is?
BOY 5   There's a rehearsal for the play, sir.
PHIL   Play rehearsal! Good God, no wonder the school's a sporting disaster. No priorities.
BOY 2   Sir, could I go and change...
PHIL   Right. Let's get going. You all know what I'm looking for...a goal scorer...and that means two things...ball control, shooting accuracy and the ability to *read the game*...three things. So this trial will allow me to assess these two...three...particular aspects of your skills. (*Phil notices one boy's feet.*) What's the idea of sandshoes, boy? No boots? (*The boy shakes his head.*)
BOY 6   I'll get some if I get the place.
PHIL   No, that's a dead loss son...there's no point in carrying on...go and get changed. We play in real boots in this school, from the word go.

(The boy wanders off to the school building.)

    Right. Simple ball control. I want you to trot with the ball at your feet, fifty yards and back...two lines...go!

(The boys do their best. Some disappear off stage. DOROTHY walks up to Phil. She is dressed in an immaculate track suit.)

    Both sides of the foot! Let me see complete control...

(Dorothy approaches the group. Phil presumes that she is on some errand or other and gives her little attention.)

    (*Shouting to boys off stage*) I want it faster now...come on...What d'you want lass? Get some pace into it! Anybody can walk with a ball...
DOT.   (*Waiting patiently*) Sir...
PHIL   What is it, dear?
DOT.   The trial. I'm here for the trial.
PHIL   This is football here sweetheart ...maybe Miss McAlpine is up to something with the hockey team, I don't know, but this here is football...boys...
DOT.   That's right. Football trials at eleven a.m. I saw the notice.
PHIL   There's been a slight misunderstanding, dear, it was boys I meant...for the trials.
DOT.   Didn't say so on the notice...just said 'talented players'.
PHIL   That's a shame you picked it up wrongly ...but I'm afraid I can't do anything now.

(The boys have given up their dribbling and have gathered round.)

DOT.   You didn't *say* boys only. You're not allowed to anyway. I want a trial.
PHIL   Not possible, dear...not today...we don't have a spare ball...We can fix something later on though, I'll talk to Miss McAlpine.

(Dorothy deftly flicks up a ball.)

DOT.   Here's one.
PHIL   (*Tries to ignore her but knows she is still there*) Two basic skills...control and...the other one. Trotting with the ball again...two lines...lots of speed...on you go.

(Dorothy joins one of the lines. Her ball control is superb. None of the boys can touch her. GREGORY, ANDY and CHARLIE are watching from the side.)

ANDY   He's not going to let her play.
GREG.   He's letting her play.
ANDY   I'm not denying I'd fancy a bit.
GREG.   Look at that control.
ANDY   What about body contact. It's a physical game.
GREG.   Body contact!
ANDY   He'll not let her play. He can't.
GREG.   She can play alright.

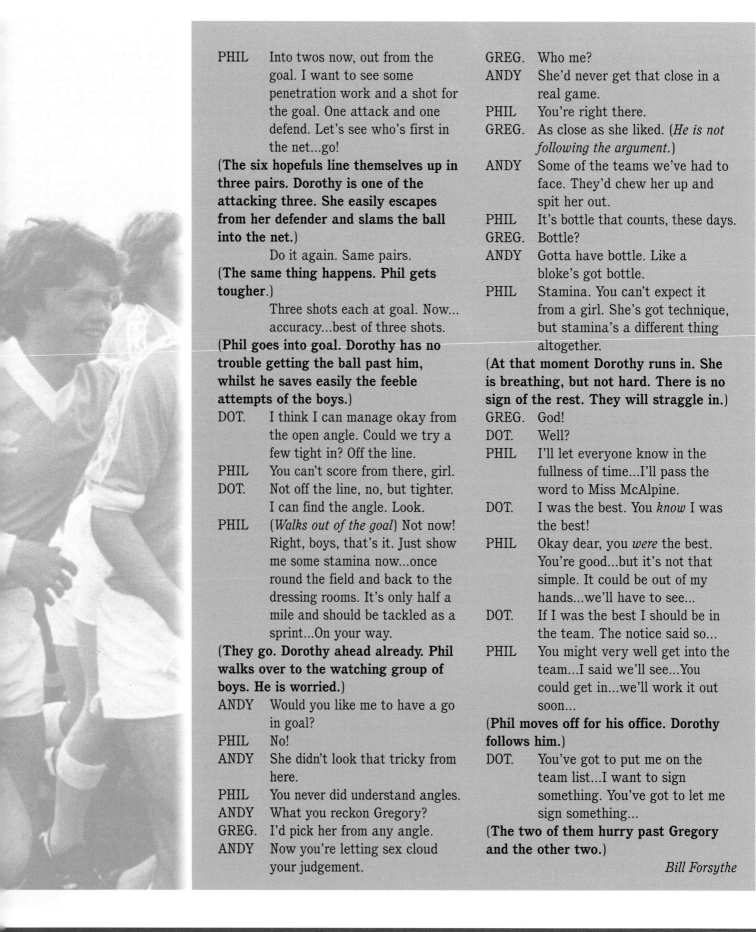

PHIL   Into twos now, out from the goal. I want to see some penetration work and a shot for the goal. One attack and one defend. Let's see who's first in the net...go!

(The six hopefuls line themselves up in three pairs. Dorothy is one of the attacking three. She easily escapes from her defender and slams the ball into the net.)

Do it again. Same pairs.

(The same thing happens. Phil gets tougher.)

Three shots each at goal. Now... accuracy...best of three shots.

(Phil goes into goal. Dorothy has no trouble getting the ball past him, whilst he saves easily the feeble attempts of the boys.)

DOT.   I think I can manage okay from the open angle. Could we try a few tight in? Off the line.

PHIL   You can't score from there, girl.

DOT.   Not off the line, no, but tighter. I can find the angle. Look.

PHIL   (*Walks out of the goal*) Not now! Right, boys, that's it. Just show me some stamina now...once round the field and back to the dressing rooms. It's only half a mile and should be tackled as a sprint...On your way.

(They go. Dorothy ahead already. Phil walks over to the watching group of boys. He is worried.)

ANDY   Would you like me to have a go in goal?

PHIL   No!

ANDY   She didn't look that tricky from here.

PHIL   You never did understand angles.

ANDY   What you reckon Gregory?

GREG.   I'd pick her from any angle.

ANDY   Now you're letting sex cloud your judgement.

GREG.   Who me?

ANDY   She'd never get that close in a real game.

PHIL   You're right there.

GREG.   As close as she liked. (*He is not following the argument.*)

ANDY   Some of the teams we've had to face. They'd chew her up and spit her out.

PHIL   It's bottle that counts, these days.

GREG.   Bottle?

ANDY   Gotta have bottle. Like a bloke's got bottle.

PHIL   Stamina. You can't expect it from a girl. She's got technique, but stamina's a different thing altogether.

(At that moment Dorothy runs in. She is breathing, but not hard. There is no sign of the rest. They will straggle in.)

GREG.   God!

DOT.   Well?

PHIL   I'll let everyone know in the fullness of time...I'll pass the word to Miss McAlpine.

DOT.   I was the best. You *know* I was the best!

PHIL   Okay dear, you *were* the best. You're good...but it's not that simple. It could be out of my hands...we'll have to see...

DOT.   If I was the best I should be in the team. The notice said so...

PHIL   You might very well get into the team...I said we'll see...You could get in...we'll work it out soon...

(Phil moves off for his office. Dorothy follows him.)

DOT.   You've got to put me on the team list...I want to sign something. You've got to let me sign something...

(The two of them hurry past Gregory and the other two.)

Bill Forsythe

TEXT LEVEL WORK

Comprehension

A 1 Why have so few boys turned up for the football trials?

2 What three things is Phil looking for in a goal scorer?

3 When Dorothy says she has come for a football trial, where does Phil suggest she should be?

4 In which three specific things does Dorothy outshine the boys?

5 What does Phil reluctantly have to admit at the end of the trial?

B 1 From the exchange between the boys at the beginning of the scene, what impression do you get of the general attitude to football in the school?

2 What, in contrast, is Phil's attitude to the game?

3 What does Andy mean when he says, '*Some of the teams we've had to face. They'd chew her up and spit her out.*'?

4 Although Phil admits that Dorothy is '*the best*', he adds '*but it's not that simple*'. What do you think he means?

C What impression does the writer create of:

- Phil
- Dorothy?

You should consider:

- their actions
- their dialogue.

WORD LEVEL WORK

Vocabulary

Dictionary and contextual work

Use a dictionary and the context of the extract to explain the meaning of the following words:

1 aspiring	5 immaculate	9 penetration
2 priorities	6 presumes	10 stamina
3 accuracy	7 misunderstanding	11 bottle
4 ability	8 deftly	12 technique

Spelling

Words ending in 'ar'

Key word: particul**ar**

1 Use this key word in a sentence of your own.

2 Learn these important 'ar' words:

familiar   peculi**ar**   simil**ar**

gramm**ar**   calend**ar**

SENTENCE LEVEL WORK

Grammar and punctuation

Subordinating conjunctions

> A **subordinating conjunction** comes at the beginning of a subordinate (dependent) clause establishing the relationship between the subordinate (dependent) clause and the rest of the sentence. The subordinate (dependent) clause depends on the rest of the sentence for its meaning.
>
> Subordinating conjunctions are words used to introduce a clause and to show that the clause that follows it is less important than the main (independent) clause, eg
>
> | | | | | |
> |---|---|---|---|---|
> | after | although | as | as if | as long as |
> | because | before | even though | if | if only |
> | in order that | once | rather than | since | so that |
> | that | though | unless | until | when |
> | whenever | where | whereas | wherever | while |

Copy these sentences and underline, colour or highlight the subordinating conjunctions.

1 We are going out to practise after the trial.
2 Since we have equal opportunities, we have got to have girls in the team.
3 While I was waiting in line for the football trial, I saw Dorothy.
4 Although the line was long, Dorothy's performance was well worth waiting for.
5 Even if you have sexist views, you will have to recognise that Dorothy's brilliant.
6 I thought Dorothy was brilliant because she is so skilful and fit.

TEXT LEVEL WORK

Writing

Play scripts

> We get a clear impression of the type of people Dorothy and Phil are from their actions and speech in the play *Gregory's Girl*. This is because playwrights:
> - have to decide what their characters are like
> - imagine how they would speak and react to situations.

Language features

Dramatic dialogue

A playwright has to think carefully about many aspects of a character's speech and decide:

- do they speak with an accent?
- do they speak in slang or standard English?
- what kind of vocabulary they use
- how they would speak in a given situation.

Actions

The actions of a character *on paper* are given in the stage directions but these must:

- be translated into realistic action on the stage
- help the audience to understand the character.

Layout

As with any play script there are conventions of layout. Play scripts will be different in their use of bold, italics, brackets etc but once a style has been decided on, it is followed consistently. In this extract:

- characters' names are in capitals, eg

  'DOROTHY'

- major stage directions are in bold and bracketed, eg

  '**(The boy wonders off to the school building.)**'

- stage directions which indicate a character's actions while speaking are in italics and bracketed, eg

  '(*Phil notices one boy's feet*)'.

Writing assignment

Write an ending for the scene where Dorothy continues to insist that Phil signs her up for the team. You should:

- keep the characters of Dorothy and Phil consistent
- follow the layout
- decide who wins the argument
- introduce another character, eg Miss McAlpine, Gregory.

Personal choice

Choose one of the following assignments.

1 Imagine you are Dorothy and you have been refused a place in the football team. Write a letter to the head teacher, explaining the situation and giving reasons why the decision should be changed.

2 Imagine you are Phil. You have refused to let Dorothy play in the team. Write an interview with the head teacher in which you justify your actions.

Angry at the world

Rebel Without a Cause, *starring James Dean, has become a cult film from the 1960s. It tells the story of a 1950s teenager, angry at the world for little apparent reason. James Dean's cult status was confirmed by his tragic early death in a road accident on the way to race his sports car. In the opening sequence of the film, we see two separate events: one, the harassment of an innocent bystander, on Christmas Eve; the other, a teenager who has been drinking and is mistakenly arrested for the harassment of the man.*

FADE IN:

A DEEP NIGHT SKY – MATTE SHOT

CAMERA SEARCHES slowly upward through the heavens and the silver tone of a bell is HEARD sounding the strokes of midnight.

On the final note of the bell, CAMERA is full on the Milky Way and there it rests, just long enough for a burst of Christmas singing to arise. The carol is sung by the crude, unmatched voices of children.

CAMERA PANS DOWN TO INCLUDE:

SPIRE OF A CHURCH

CAMERA continues its DOWNWARD PAN and we pass a window behind which is the source of the singing. CAMERA PANS OFF WINDOW TO SHOW – LONG SHOT – CITY – NIGHT

Suddenly revealed – crisp and sparkling with lights and framed by a lighted Christmas tree. CAMERA PANS DOWN AND OVER:

A LONELY STREET FULL OF PARKED CARS

The singing diminishes but a thread of it remains. A car has just parked. The headlights snap off. A MAN emerges whistling the same Christmas melody and pulls some gifts from the front seat. He slams the door and starts down the street in the direction of a house with bright windows. He must pass an empty lot full of rusty grass and litter which lies in darkness between two streetlights.

As the Man walks by the lot, still whistling, a GROUP OF FIGURES rises silently from the grass, figures who have been lying in concealment until now. They step noiselessly onto the pavement and follow the Man. At the sound of their boots the whistling stops. The Man glances behind him and sees the figures walking after him, filling the pavement. A streetlight shows them to be boys and girls and all quite young. The Man moves on more swiftly and the sound of their pursuit increases. He begins to run TOWARD the lighted house and the following footsteps run too. Suddenly he stops under the next streetlight and turns to face the figures. They are upon him and around him quickly. Nobody speaks for a moment, then one of the boys grins. His name is BUZZ. He is big and filled with an awareness of his own masculinity.

> BUZZ (*Friendly, cool*)
> That was pretty what you were whistling. Whistle some more.

The Man whistles a nervous phrase, trying to make a joke of the situation which he doesn't understand.

> BUZZ (*Suddenly*)
> You got a cigarette?

> MAN
> Oh, I think so –

The Man fumbles in his pocket, finds a pack and drops it in his nervousness. The figures wait until he picks it up. He offers one to Buzz.

> MAN
> Filter tips.

> BUZZ (*Smiling – encouraging*)
> You smoke it. Smoke it, Dad.

Smiling uncertainly, the Man puts the cigarette in his mouth. Buzz, still smiling, takes out a packet of wooden matches.

> BUZZ
> I'll light it for you, Dad.

Buzz ignites a match and holds it near the Man's face for a second, searching it. Then he lights the whole box under his nose. The Man shrieks, and his packages fall. Buzz slaps him sharply, his smile gone.

> MAN (*Shrieking*)
> It's Christmas!

The CAMERA PANS AWAY as the figures enclose him, and HOLDS on a small mechanical monkey which has dropped from its wrappings. It begins to dance madly on the pavement, then runs down.

The feet of the figures scatter past the unmoving monkey. Then CAMERA RISES to SHOW that the Man has disappeared. There is a moment of awful stillness, then we see a boy coming down the street alone. He is quite drunk, and he slips once. This is JIM, a good-looking kid of seventeen with a crew-cut and wearing a good suit. The spilled packages on the pavement stop him. He bends down to see what they are and picks up the mechanical monkey from the wreckage. He smiles and winds it up. He sets it on the sidewalk and sits down. He watches it dance for a moment, happily. A siren is HEARD distantly, growing louder. Jim pays no attention to it as he winds the monkey again and releases it for its dance.

SUPERIMPOSE TITLE:
'REBEL WITHOUT A CAUSE'
As SIREN rises piercingly close, and Jim looks up, we DISSOLVE TO:

CLOSE SHOT – THROBBING LIGHT OF POLICE CAR – NIGHT
The siren SCREAMING wildly, then dying. The SOUND of brakes. CAMERA MOVES TO REVEAL the police car stopped at the entrance of a Precinct Station. Two OFFICERS dismount, bearing between them the struggling Jim. They bear him up the steps and in through the double doors.

TEXT LEVEL WORK

Comprehension

A 1 What two sound effects begin the opening sequence of the film?

2 What is the opening camera shot of the film?

3 What toy was the man in the opening sequence taking home?

4 How old is Jim?

5 What two sound effects end the opening sequence of the film?

B 1 Explain the following in your own words:

    a '... *crude, unmatched voices of children ...*'
    b '... *headlights snap off ...*'
    c '... *an empty lot full of rusty grass and litter ...*'.

2 Which details from the script reveal that it is Christmas? Quote from the extract in support of your views.

3 What do you learn from the description of the toy, when it says:
'*It begins to dance madly on the pavement, then runs down.*'?

4 Why do you think the script includes the sounds of the children singing Christmas carols?

C Using evidence from the text, what can you infer about the way the writer attempts to create a sympathetic impression of Jim's character and an unsympathetic impression of Buzz? You should comment on:

- stage directions
- movements, gestures or actions
- dialogue
- language.

WORD LEVEL WORK

Vocabulary

Dictionary and contextual work

Use a dictionary and the context of the passage to explain the meaning of the following words:

1 spire	4 concealment	7 masculinity	10 wreckage
2 diminishes	5 pavement	8 ignites	11 siren
3 melody	6 pursuit	9 mechanical	12 precinct

Spelling

'us' words

Key word: stat**us**

1 Use the key word in a sentence of your own.

2 Learn these important 'us' words:

vir**us**   min**us**   radi**us**   thesaur**us**

SENTENCE LEVEL WORK

Grammar and punctuation

Punctuation revisited

Punctuation marks are signs to alert readers, which would be suggested in speech by pauses or changes in tone of voice.

The **semicolon** is used:
- to join related independent clauses in compound sentences
- to separate items in a list if it already includes commas.

A **colon** is used:
- to introduce one or more directly related ideas after a complete statement, eg a list, a series of directions, or a quotation illustrating or explaining the statement
- in a business letter greeting
- between the hour and minutes in time
- between chapter and verse in biblical references.

Parentheses or brackets are used:
- for non-essential material in a sentence, eg dates, sources.

A **dash** is used:
- to emphasise a point
- to introduce an explanatory comment.

Quotation marks are used:
- to indicate direct quotations
- to indicate words used ironically, or in some unusual way.

Underlining and italics are used:
- to indicate titles, eg books, newspapers, films
- for foreign words that are not common in English
- for words or phrases that need emphasis.

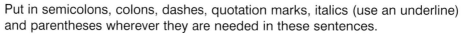

Put in semicolons, colons, dashes, quotation marks, italics (use an underline) and parentheses wherever they are needed in these sentences.

1 The people in question Buzz, the other youths and Jim represent typical teenagers.

2 Several people took part in the harassment of the man Buzz, some male youths, some females, but not Jim.

3 Only one course of action seemed appropriate to me, said the man who had been assaulted, and I ran.

4 Jim later to be arrested had been drinking excessively.

5 In the police station, as a result of mistaken identity, Jim was treated as if he was a criminal photographed and fingerprinted.

6 Yes, Jim said, I was there about midnight.

7 There was only one thing to do in the circumstances phone Jim's parents.

8 Jim said teenagers are always blamed in this town.

9 The following were found near the scene of the crime packages, wrapping paper and a mechanical monkey.

10 Arriving at the police station were a police car, the man who'd been assaulted, two police officers and Jim, the suspect.

TEXT LEVEL WORK

Writing

Writing screenplays

> Screenplays are one of the most efficient ways of writing a narrative unit, scene by scene. The effectiveness of a scene is determined by its length, so the beginning and the ending of the scene are crucial. Another key to successful screenplays is to write effective action. This extract, from the screenplay of *Rebel Without a Cause*, uses all these elements effectively.

Language features

Beginning a scene
The story determines what details you need to show. Too much detail doesn't move the story forward.

Don't waste time describing the beginning of the scene. Start straight into the action, where new story information begins to be revealed, eg

> 'The headlights snap off.'

Ending a scene
End a scene:

- with a 'punch line' or a moment that raises questions
- when a dynamic new element is added to the drama
- in a way that surprises the audience, eg

> 'Two OFFICERS dismount, bearing between them the struggling Jim. They bear him up the steps and in through the double doors.'

Transitions

To write effectively, you need to make the changes from one scene into the next scene (called *transitions*) tight and dramatic. End a scene when its point is made and begin the next scene by moving straight into an action, which moves the story forward, eg

'*The siren SCREAMING wildly, then dying. The SOUND of brakes.*'

Action

Fiction writers describe everything in detail in order to create a clear impression of what is happening for the reader. The screenwriter writes general suggestions, eg

'*FADE IN:*
A DEEP NIGHT SKY – MATTE SHOT
CAMERA SEARCHES ...'.

The job of the screenwriter is to tell the story, directly and simply:

* by telling us what we see on the screen, eg SPIRE OF A CHURCH
* by telling us what we hear in dialogue and other sound effects, eg

'*... burst of Christmas singing*'.

Focus on story movement and action. Avoid explaining information, instead communicate on the screen, through action or dialogue. Use 'white space' to direct the visual movement of the story. A paragraph in a screenplay is like an individual camera shot set-up.

Language choices

Writers make conscious choices of language:

* to imply meaning, eg

'*That was pretty what you were whistling. Whistle some more.*'
Here, the use of the imperative '*Whistle some more*' suggests that there is more going on than just a request to hear a pretty tune.

* to establish the tone, eg

'*BUZZ (Suddenly)*
You got a cigarette?'
Here, the stage direction and the lack of politeness in the question suggest a tone of aggression.

Writing assignment

Write a screenplay of two scenes, in which a crime takes place, but mistaken identity results in the wrong person being arrested. Use the information given in the language features to help you. You should consider:

* scene beginnings
* scene endings
* transitions from one scene to the next
* action
* language choices.

Personal choice

Choose one of the following assignments.

1 Draw the storyboard for the screenplay extract from *Rebel Without a Cause*.

2 Write a statement for the police, explaining what happened in the opening sequence of *Rebel Without a Cause*, as if you were a bystander.

Oh my name it is nothin'.

Youthful rebellion during the 1960s took many forms but one of the most popular was in the lyrics of pop music. One particular type of pop music, which was associated with rebellion against the authorities of the day, was the 'protest song'. A leading figure in the writing of protest songs was the American folk singer, Bob Dylan. His lyrics were often ironic and scathing about government, the churches and other public institutions.

Oh my name it is nothin'
My age it means less
The country I come from
Is called the Midwest
I's taught and brought up there
The laws to abide
And that land that I live in
Has God on its side.

Oh the history books tell it
They tell it so well
The cavalries charged
The Indians fell
The cavalries charged
The Indians died
Oh the country was young
With God on its side.

Oh the Spanish-American
War had its day
And the Civil War too
Was soon laid away
And the names of the heroes
I's made to memorize
With guns in their hands
And God on their side.

Oh the First World War, boys
It closed out its fate
The reason for fighting
I never got straight
But I learned to accept it
Accept it with pride
For you don't count the dead
When God's on your side.

When the Second World War
Came to an end
We forgave the Germans
And we were friends
Though they murdered six million
In the ovens they fried
The Germans now too
Have God on their side.

I've learned to hate Russians
All through my whole life
If another war starts
It's them we must fight
To hate them and fear them
To run and to hide
And accept it all bravely
With God on my side.

But now we got weapons
Of the chemical dust
If fire them we're forced to
Then fire them we must
One push of the button
And a shot the world wide
And you never ask questions
When God's on your side.

In many a dark hour
I've been thinkin' about this
That Jesus Christ
Was betrayed by a kiss
But I can't think for you
You'll have to decide
Whether Judas Iscariot
Had God on his side.

So now as I'm leavin'
I'm weary as Hell
The confusion I'm feelin'
Ain't no tongue can tell
The words fill my head
And fall to the floor
If God's on our side
He'll stop the next war.

Bob Dylan

TEXT LEVEL WORK

Comprehension

A 1 Where was Bob Dylan born and educated, according to the song?

2 Name two American wars mentioned in the song.

3 Which two nationalities does the song name, as enemies of America?

4 Who was Judas Iscariot?

5 Who were the '*murdered six million*' mentioned in the song?

B 1 Explain the following in your own words:

a '*The laws to abide*'
b '*the names of the heroes
   I's made to memorize.*'
c '*And a shot the world wide*'.

2 Which details from the song reveal that Bob Dylan was opposed to war? Quote from the extract in support of your views.

3 What do you learn from the song, when it says:
'*The cavalries charged
The Indians died
Oh the country was young
With God on its side*'?

4 Why do you think the song includes the words:
'*The reason for fighting
I never got straight
But I learned to accept it
Accept it with pride*'?

C Using evidence from the text, what can you infer about the writer's ironic tone in the song? You should comment on:
- the structure of the song
- the final lines of the verses
- modern history
- the writer's viewpoint.

WORD LEVEL WORK

Vocabulary

Dictionary and contextual work

Use a dictionary and the context of the passage to explain the meaning of the following words:

1 rebellion	5 ironic	9 cavalry
2 youthful	6 scathing	10 betrayed
3 lyrics	7 government	11 confusion
4 protest	8 institutions	12 tongue

Spelling

Double 'c' words

Key word: a**cc**ept

1 Use the key word in a sentence of your own.

2 Learn these important double 'c' words:

a**cc**ommodation   o**cc**asion   su**cc**ess   a**cc**ident

SENTENCE LEVEL WORK

Grammar and punctuation

Apostrophes

- Use the apostrophe with contractions, placing it where the letter(s) has been removed, eg

    Can **no**t = can't

- Use the apostrophe before the 's' to show possession by one person, eg

    The man**'s** car.

- Make the noun plural first then use the apostrophe to show possession by more than one person, eg

    All the car**s'** boots were open.

- If two people possess the same item, only use the apostrophe and 's' after the second name, eg

    Mike and Alison**'s** house is constructed of cob and thatch.

- Never use an apostrophe with possessive pronouns – 'its', 'his', 'hers', 'theirs', 'ours', 'yours' – these already show possession so do not need an apostrophe, eg

    The dog has hurt **its** paw.

Copy and complete these sentences, placing apostrophes where they are needed.

1 The cavalrys charge killed many Indians.

2 The heroes names were memorised by pupils. (More than one hero.)

3 The womens clothing is on the first floor.

4 Its a shame that so many people have died.

5 Gods on our side, according to the song.

6 The Holocaust resulted in six million Jews deaths.

7 Childrens minds were taught to hate the Russians.

8 Are the words in Dylans song his own?

9 Youre right to be confused when youre trying to make sense of history.

10 The pointless waste of young lives in war is one of its horrors.

TEXT LEVEL WORK

Writing

Writing protest songs/poetry

Songs and poetry create patterns of language that make powerful use of sound and images. Protest songs and poetry express their writer's strong views on contemporary issues. The late 1960s and the early 1970s saw protest music and poetry reach its greatest influence. The American involvement in the Vietnam War and the Civil Rights Movement gave musicians and poets a great deal to sing and write about. Bob Dylan emerged in New York in the 1960s as a rebel folksinger who wrote songs the likes of which hadn't been heard before. There were quite a few other singer-songwriters who were singing protest songs, most of them following the genre established by Woody Guthrie, the American folk singer. Dylan's songs/poetry challenged conservative attitudes to politics and society, posing thoughtful questions about human and civil rights, and demanding justice.

Language features

Rhythm

By carrying out a syllable count, it is clear that the song has an easy flow and sense of rhythm, eg

Verse		
	1	7, 5, 6, 5, 6, 5, 7, 5
	2	7, 5, 5, 5, 5, 5, 6, 5
	3	7, 4, 6, 5, 7, 5, 5, 5
	4	6, 5, 6, 5, 7, 5, 6, 5
	5	6, 4, 6, 4, 7, 6, 5, 5
	6	6, 5, 5, 5, 6, 5, 7, 5
	7	6, 6, 6, 5, 6, 6, 7, 5
	8	6, 7, 4, 6, 6, 5, 7, 5
	9	6, 5, 7, 5, 5, 5, 5, 5

There are clear patterns of line length – long lines being slower in pace, and short lines being fast paced – the overall pace of the song being upbeat.

Sound effects

Rhyme, alliteration, assonance and repetition are used for effect.

- Rhyme – Dylan uses pairs of regular alternating rhyme, ababcdcd, which provides a consistent meter.
- Alliteration – is where a particular consonant sound is repeated, eg

    '*Ain't no tongue can **tell**'*.

Here, the letter 't' is emphasised. As this letter is a dental sound, made by putting the teeth together, it tends to fragment or break up the flow of the lines.

Another example is found in the lines:
    '***If** **f**ire the**m** we're **f**orced to*
    *Then **f**ire the**m** we **m**ust*'.

In these lines the emphasis is on the letter 'f' (a sibilant/hissing sound) and the letter 'm' (a nasal sound). Both of these sounds enhance the flow of the lines.

- Assonance – is where a particular vowel sound is repeated, eg

    '*The country I come from*'.

    In this line, the letter 'o' is emphasised but saying a short 'u' sound, which tends to increase the fluency of the line.

- Repetition – is used to create a rhythmic or 'echo' effect, suggesting a to and fro movement, eg

    '*The cavalries charged
    The Indians fell
    The cavalries charged
    The Indians died*'.

Narrative voice

The narrative voice sounds ironic in tone, within its context, eg

'*I've learned to hate Russians
All through my whole life*'.

Dylan expresses the common experience of a young American living through the Cold War of the 1960s.

Figurative language

The writer uses:

- hyperbole (pronounced 'hi-per-boll-ee' and meaning gross exaggeration), eg
    '*Oh my name it is nothin'
    My age it means less*'.
    His age can hardly be less than nothing!

- personification (giving a non-human object the behaviour of a live thing), eg
    '*Oh the history books tell it*'.
    Here, the books are *behaving* like something alive, telling a story.

- metaphor (a comparison between qualities of dissimilar objects), eg
    '*Oh the country was young*'.
    Here, the country is being compared with a living creature, in terms of a lifetime – young, middle-aged, old.

- simile (a comparison that uses the words 'like' or 'as'), eg
    '*I'm weary as Hell*'.
    Here, the narrator is comparing how he feels with the imagined exhaustion felt by somebody in Hell, using the word 'as'.

Writing assignment

Write a song or poem protesting about something that you feel strongly about, eg relationships, parents, school, animal rights etc. Use the language features to help you. You should consider:

- rhythm patterns
- sound effects
- narrative voice
- figurative language.

Personal choice

Choose one of the following assignments.

1 Write an argumentative essay, expressing your views on an issue that you feel strongly about.

2 Research and make notes on the lyrics of other protest songs by Bob Dylan, eg *Masters of War*, *The Times They Are A-Changin'*.

you deserve to be taught a lesson

In his novel of the near future, A Clockwork Orange, *Anthony Burgess describes the aggression, drug-taking and vandalism of a group of teenagers. The central character, an anti-hero called Alex, is intelligent and sensitive in his own way but he is rebelling against the controls of the society he lives in and takes pleasure in violence against others.*

So we scatted out into the big winter nochy and walked down Marghanita Boulevard and then turned into Boothby Avenue, and there we found what we were pretty well looking for, a malenky jest to start off the evening with. There was a doddery starry schoolmaster type veck, glasses on and his rot open to the cold nochy air. He had books under his arm and a crappy umbrella and was coming round the corner from the Public Biblio, which not many lewdies used those days. You never really saw many of the older bourgeois type out after nightfall those days, what with the shortage of police and we fine young malchickiwicks about, and this prof type chelloveck was the only one walking in the whole of the street. So we goolied up to him, very polite, and I said: 'Pardon me, brother.'

He looked a malenky bit poogly when he viddied the four of us like that, coming up so quiet and polite and smiling, but he said: 'Yes? What is it?' in a very loud teacher-type goloss, as if he was trying to show us he wasn't poogly. I said:

'I see you have books under your arm, brother. It is indeed a rare pleasure these days to come across somebody that still reads, brother.'

'Oh,' he said, all shaky. 'Is it? Oh, I see.' And he kept looking from one to the other of we four, finding himself now like in the middle of a very smiling and polite square.

'Yes,' I said. 'It would interest me greatly, brother, if you would kindly allow me to see what books those are that you have under your arm. I like nothing better in this world than a good clean book, brother.'

'Clean,' he said. 'Clean, eh?' And then Pete skvatted these three books from him and handed them round real skorry. Being three, we all had one each to viddy at except for Dim. The one I had was called *Elementary Crystallography*, so I opened it up and said: 'Excellent, really first-class,' keeping turning the pages. Then I said in a very shocked type goloss: 'But what is this here? What is this filthy slovo, I blush to look at this word. You disappoint me, brother, you do really.'

'But,' he tried, 'but, but.'

'Now,' said Georgie, 'here is what I should call real dirt. There's one slovo beginning with an f and another with a c.' He had a book called *The Miracle of the Snowflake*.

'Oh,' said poor old Dim, smotting over Pete's shoulder and going too far, like he always did, 'it says here what he done to her, and there's a picture and all. Why,' he said, 'you're nothing but a filthy-minded old skitebird.'

'An old man of your age, brother,' I said, and I started to rip up the book I'd got, and the others did the same with the ones they had, Dim and Pete doing a tug-of-war with *The Rhombohedral System*. The starry prof type began to creech: 'But those are not mine, those are the property of the municipality, this is sheer wantonness and vandal work,' or some such slovos. And he tried to sort of wrest the books back off of us, which was like pathetic. 'You deserve to be taught a lesson, brother,' I said, 'that you do.' This crystal book I had was very tough-bound and hard to razrez to bits, being real starry and made in days when things were made to last like, but I managed to rip the pages up and chuck them in handfuls of like snowflakes, though big, all over this creeching old veck, and then the others did the same with theirs, old Dim just dancing about like the clown he was.

'There you are,' said Pete. 'There's the mackerel of the cornflake for you, you dirty reader of filth and nastiness.'

'You naughty old veck, you,' I said, and then we began to filly about with him. Pete held his rookers and Georgie sort of hooked his rot wide open for him and Dim yanked out his false zoobies, upper and lower. He threw these down on the pavement and then I treated them to the old boot-crush, though they were hard b******* like, being made of some new horrorshow plastic stuff. The old veck began to make sort of chumbling shooms – 'wuf waf wof' – so Georgie let go of holding his goobers apart and just let him have one in the toothless rot with his ringy fist, and that made the old veck start moaning a lot then, then out comes the blood, my brothers, real beautiful. So all we did then was to pull his outer platties off, stripping him down to his vest and long underpants (very starry; Dim smecked his head off near), and then Pete kicks him lovely in his pot, and we let him go. He went sort of staggering off, it not having been too hard of a tolchock really, going 'Oh oh oh', not knowing where or what was what really, and we had a snigger at him and then riffled through his pockets, Dim dancing round with his crappy umbrella meanwhile, but there wasn't much in them. There were a few starry letters, some of them dating right back to 1960 with 'My dearest dearest' in them and all that chepooka, and a keyring and a starry leaky pen. Old Dim gave up his umbrella dance and of course had to start reading one of the letters out loud, like to show the empty street he could read. 'My darling one,' he recited, in this very high type goloss, 'I shall be thinking of you while you are away and hope you will remember to wrap up warm when you go out at night.' Then he let out a very shoomny smeck – 'Ho ho ho' – pretending to start wiping his yahma with it. 'All right,' I said. 'Let it go, O my brothers.' In the trousers of this starry veck there was only a malenky bit of cutter (money, that is) – not more than three gollies – so we gave all his messy little coin the scatter treatment, it being hen-korm to the amount of pretty polly we had on us already. Then we smashed the umbrella and razrezzed his platties and gave them to the blowing winds, my brothers, and then we'd finished with the starry teacher type veck. We hadn't done much, I know, but that was only like the start of the evening and I make no appy polly loggies to thee or thine for that. The knives in the milk plus were stabbing away nice and horrorshow now.

Anthony Burgess

TEXT LEVEL WORK

Comprehension

A 1 What were the names of the four youths in the extract?

2 Who did the youths assault?

3 Where had the youths' victim been, before the assault?

4 Name the three books that the victim was carrying.

5 Name three things that the victim had in his possession, apart from the books.

B 1 Explain the following in your own words:

  a 'I make no appy polly loggies ...'
  b '... new horrorshow plastic stuff ...'
  c '... holding his goobers apart ...'.
  d '... his ringy fist ...'
  e '... pull his outer platties off ...'
  f '... smecked his head off ...'
  g '... not having been too hard of a tolchock ...'.

2 Why did the writer include this incident with the letters:

  'There were a few starry letters, some of them dating right back to 1960'?

Quote from the extract in support of your views.

3 What do you learn from the extract, when it says:

  'The knives in the milk plus were stabbing away nice and horrorshow now'?

4 Why do you think the youths assault their victim? Comment on their motivation, referring to evidence, eg

  '... there was only a malenky bit of cutter (money, that is) – not more than three gollies – so we gave all his messy little coin the scatter treatment, it being hen-korm to the amount of pretty polly we had on us already.'

C Using evidence from the text, what can you infer about the narrator? You should comment on:

- his character
- his use of language
- his tone
- his viewpoint and attitudes.

WORD LEVEL WORK

Vocabulary

Dictionary and contextual work
Use a dictionary and the context of the passage to explain the meaning of the following words:

1 aggression	5 bourgeois	9 municipality
2 vandalism	6 elementary	10 wrest
3 boulevard	7 crystallography	11 pathetic
4 avenue	8 rhombohedral	12 tongue

Spelling

'graph' words
Key word: crystallo**graph**y

  1 Use the key word in a sentence of your own.

  2 Learn these important 'graph' words:

  graph   geo**graph**y   **graph**ite   **graph**ic

SENTENCE LEVEL WORK

Grammar and punctuation

Invented language

Anthony Burgess is only one of many writers who have invented their own words, when creating a fictional world. Many of his words are adapted from other languages. Yet, the way the language is structured often enables the reader to work out what the unfamiliar words mean.

Copy the table and, using the context of the extract, write your own dictionary definitions for these words. In your definitions, suggest where the words might have their origins, eg in Russian, or the name of a bird, etc.

Word	Definition and origin
chelloveck	
creech	
goloss	
goolied	
lewdies	
malchickiwicks	
malenky	
nochy	
poogly	
razrez	
rookers	
rot	
skitebird	
skorry	
skvatted	
slovo	
starry	
veck	
viddied	
zoobies	

TEXT LEVEL WORK

Writing

Inventing a language

A number of writers have invented new language, when they wished:

- to create an imaginary world
- to change the reader's reactions to a character
- to establish an unusual mood
- to make the reader question how and why we say things as we do.

Lewis Carroll wrote nonsense language in *Jabberwocky*, eg

''Twas brillig and the slithy toves did gyre and gimbal in the wabe'.

James Joyce also wrote in an odd way in *Finnegan's Wake*, eg

'The great fall of the offwall entailed at such short notice the pftjschute of Finnegan, erse solid man, that the humptyhillhead of humself promptly sends an unquiring one well to the west in quest of his tumptytumtoes: and their upturnpikepointandplace is at the knock out in the park where oranges have been laid to rust upon the green since devlinsfirst loved livvy.'

Fantasy literature is filled with invented language, as writers develop new worlds and alien characters. An influential writer who did this was J R R Tolkien in *The Lord of the Rings*, where he used his knowledge of Anglo-Saxon, Celtic and Norse to create new languages for the orcs, dwarves and elves, eg

'GALADRIEL: I amar prestar aen, han mathon ne nen, han mathon ne chae a han noston ned 'wilith.'

This may be translated as:

'The world is changed; I can feel it in the water, I can feel it in the earth, I can smell it in the air.'

Language features
When writers create their own languages, they need to use the same sort of structures and parts of speech that we would use in our own language.

Nouns
For example: **nochy** *n.* 'night';   **Goloss** *n.* 'voice'

Adjectives
For example: **malenky** *adj.* 'little';   **poogly** *adj.* 'scared', 'anxious' or 'frightened'

Verbs
For example: **goolied** *inf.* 'sidled';   **viddy** *inf.* 'to see' or 'to look'

Adverbs
For example: **skorry** *adv.* 'quickly'

Rhythm and tone
A Clockwork Orange used Russian-based vocabulary to create the cadence and rhythms that Burgess desired. James Joyce used phonetic writing (spelling words as they sound) to imitate accent and dialect. Lewis Carroll made up nonsense words but consciously used alliteration and assonance to create the rhythms and tones that he wanted.

Writing assignment
Write a prose passage describing an imaginary confrontation between a small group of youths and a victim, with a first-person narrator. Blend new words of your own invention with standard English. You may choose to use some of the language features from *A Clockwork Orange*, if it is appropriate for your setting and characters.

Personal choice
Choose one of the following assignments.

1 Write the statement made to the police by the old man who was the victim of the assault in *A Clockwork Orange*. Use as much of the invented language as you can.

2 Research, make notes then compile a dictionary of the language invented by Anthony Burgess for *A Clockwork Orange*.

Comrades

The animals at Manor Farm rise up against their cruel owner, Mr Jones, and run him off the farm. They decide they will run the farm themselves and that all the animals will do equal work and receive equal rewards. Never again will they allow one person (or animal) to make their lives miserable.

The animals had their breakfast, and then Snowball and Napoleon called them together again. 'Comrades,' said Snowball, 'it is half-past six and we have a long day before us. Today we begin the hay harvest. But there is another matter that must be attended to first.'

The pigs now revealed that during the past three months they had taught themselves to read and write from an old spelling book which had belonged to Mr Jones' children and which had been thrown on the rubbish heap. Napoleon sent for pots of black and white paint and led the way down to the five-barred gate on to the main road. Then Snowball (for it was Snowball who was best at writing) took a brush between the two knuckles of his trotter, painted out MANOR FARM from the top bar of the gate and in its place painted ANIMAL FARM. This was to be the name of the farm from now onwards. After this they went back to the farm buildings, where Snowball and Napoleon sent for a ladder which they caused to be set against the end wall of the big barn. They explained that by their studies of the past three months the pigs had succeeded in reducing the principles of Animalism to Seven Commandments. These Seven Commandments would now be inscribed on the wall; they would form an unalterable law by which all the animals on Animal Farm must live for ever after. With some difficulty (for it is not easy for a pig to balance himself on a ladder) Snowball climbed up and set to work, with Squealer a few rungs below him holding the paint-pot. The Commandments were written on the tarred wall in great white letters that could be read thirty yards away. They ran thus:

THE SEVEN COMMANDMENTS

1 *Whatever goes upon two legs is an enemy.*

2 *Whatever goes upon four legs, or has wings, is a friend.*

3 *No animal shall wear clothes.*

4 *No animal shall sleep in a bed.*

5 *No animal shall drink alcohol.*

6 *No animal shall kill any other animal.*

7 *All animals are equal.*

... One day in early summer Squealer ordered the sheep to follow him, and led them out to a piece of waste ground at the other end of the farm, which had become overgrown with birch saplings. The sheep spent the whole day there browsing at the leaves under Squealer's supervision. In the evening he returned to the farmhouse himself, but, as it was warm weather, told the sheep to stay where they were. It ended by their remaining there for a whole week, during which time the other animals saw nothing of them. Squealer was with them for the greater part of every day. He was, he said, teaching them to sing a new song, for which privacy was needed.

It was just after the sheep had returned, on a pleasant evening when the animals had finished work and were making their way back to the farm buildings, that the terrified neighing of a horse sounded from the yard. Startled, the animals stopped in their tracks. It was Clover's voice. She neighed again, and all the animals broke into a gallop and rushed into the yard. Then they saw what Clover has seen.

It was a pig walking on his hind legs.

Yes, it was Squealer. A little awkwardly, as though not quite used to supporting his considerable bulk in that position, but with perfect balance, he was strolling across the yard. And, a moment later, out from the door of the farmhouse came a long file of pigs, all walking on their hind legs. Some did it better than others, one or two were even a trifle unsteady and looked as though they would have liked the support of a stick, but every one of them made his way right round the yard successfully. And finally there was a tremendous baying of dogs and a shrill crowing from the black cockerel, and out came Napoleon himself, majestically upright, casting haughty glances from side to side, and with his dogs gambolling round him.

He carried a whip in his trotter.

There was a deadly silence. Amazed, terrified, huddling together, the animals watched the long line of pigs march slowly round the yard. It was as though the world had turned upside-down. Then there came a moment when the first shock had worn off and when, in spite of everything – in spite of their terror of the dogs, and the habit, developed through long years, of never complaining, never criticising, no matter what happened – they might have uttered some word of protest. But just at that moment, as though at a signal, all the sheep burst out into a tremendous bleating of –

'Four legs good, two legs *better*! Four legs good, two legs *better*! Four legs good, two legs *better*!'

It went on five minutes without stopping. And by the time the sheep had quieted down, the chance to utter any protest had passed, for the pigs had marched back into the farmhouse.

Benjamin felt a nose nuzzling at his shoulder. He looked round. It was Clover. Her old eyes looked dimmer than ever. Without saying anything, she tugged gently at his mane and led him round to the end of the big barn, where the Seven Commandments were written. For a minute or two they stood gazing at the tarred wall with its white lettering.

'My sight is failing,' she said finally. 'Even when I was young I could not have read what was written there. But it appears to me that that wall looks different. Are the Seven Commandments the same as they used to be, Benjamin?'

For once Benjamin consented to break his rule, and he read out to her what was written on the wall. There was nothing there now except a single Commandment. It ran:

ALL ANIMALS ARE EQUAL
BUT SOME ARE MORE EQUAL
THAN OTHERS

George Orwell

TEXT LEVEL WORK

Comprehension

A 1 What had the pigs been doing during the last three months?

2 Where did the pigs inscribe the Seven Commandments?

3 Who supervised the sheep on '*the piece of waste ground at the other end of the farm*'?

4 At what event were the animals '*Amazed, terrified, huddling together*'?

5 What had the Seven Commandments been reduced to?

B 1 In your own words explain what kind of community the Seven Commandments described.

2 What is the first occasion which rouses the suspicion of the reader that the pigs are 'up to something'?

3 What is the significance of:
a the pigs walking on two legs
b Napoleon carrying a whip?

4 What was Squealer's intention in teaching the sheep to sing the song '*Four legs good, two legs better*'?

C What do you think the writer is trying to say about how humans behave to one another? You should consider:

- how the animals behave after Mr Jones is thrown out
- why they behave that way
- the action of the pigs
- the change in the Seven Commandments.

WORD LEVEL WORK

Vocabulary

Dictionary and contextual work
Use a dictionary and the context of the extract to explain the meaning of the following words:

1 comrades	5 unalterable	9 haughty
2 revealed	6 supervision	10 consented
3 principles	7 considerable	
4 inscribed	8 majestically	

Spelling

'au' words
Key words: **tau**ght   **cau**sed   h**au**ghty

1 Use these key words in sentences of your own.

2 Learn these important 'au' words:

authority   **Au**gust   **au**tumn
cl**au**se   f**au**lt

SENTENCE LEVEL WORK

Grammar and punctuation

Direct speech

Direct speech records the actual words spoken by someone.

Punctuation marks (known as speech marks or inverted commas) show when someone is talking. You will see them written in books as

- double inverted commas: "words spoken"
- single inverted commas: 'words spoken'.

Rules:

1 Inverted commas are put before and after the spoken words, eg

'Can you read?'

2 Always use a capital letter when someone starts to speak, eg

'**C**an you read?'

3 Any words not actually spoken remain outside the inverted commas, eg

'Today we begin the hay harvest,' **said Snowball**.

4 The punctuation of the words spoken comes inside the inverted commas, eg

'Today we begin the hay harvest**,**' said Snowball.

Copy these sentences and put the speech marks, and any other punctuation that is needed, in the correct places. Watch out for any questions or exclamations.

1 hello clover said benjamin
2 you look tired said clover
3 can you read the seven commandments asked clover
4 benjamin broke his rule and read all animals are equal but some are more equal than others
5 follow me ordered squealer
6 the sheep bleated four legs good two legs better

TEXT LEVEL WORK

Writing

Fables

Animal Farm is a modern fable. Orwell examines how the idea of 'all men being equal' would probably turn out in reality. Fables are one form of allegory where talking animals are used to convey the writer's message.

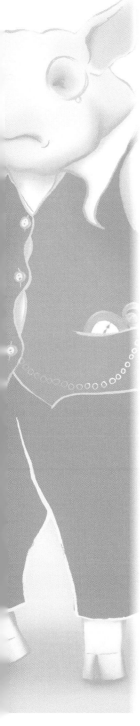

Language features

Style and language

Allegorical style is usually simple and straightforward. The story works on the level of just being a simple story but the reader has to be able to understand the 'message' easily.

Dialogue

As a main feature of a fable is the fact that animals speak, dialogue is used for characterisation and to carry the plot forward.

Symbolism

In allegories, things stand for or 'symbolise' other things. In *Animal Farm* the symbolism is as follows:

- the animals – humans
- Manor Farm/Animal Farm – a country or state which has changed its ruler by force
- the pigs – those humans who seek power over others
- the other animals – people who are ruled/subjugated by others
- the Seven Commandments – the main ideas of Communism.

Writing assignment

Using animals as characters, write a story to illustrate one of the following:

- one good turn deserves another
- look before you leap
- honesty is the best policy.

Personal choice

Choose one of the following assignments.

1 Relate the event where the pigs walked in the yard from the point of view of Clover the horse.

2 Write a scene in the farmhouse where Napoleon, Squealer, Snowball and the other pigs devise the plan of teaching the sheep the new song and walking in the yard to show that they have taken power. Show through the dramatic dialogue which of the pigs is the most powerful and gets his own way.

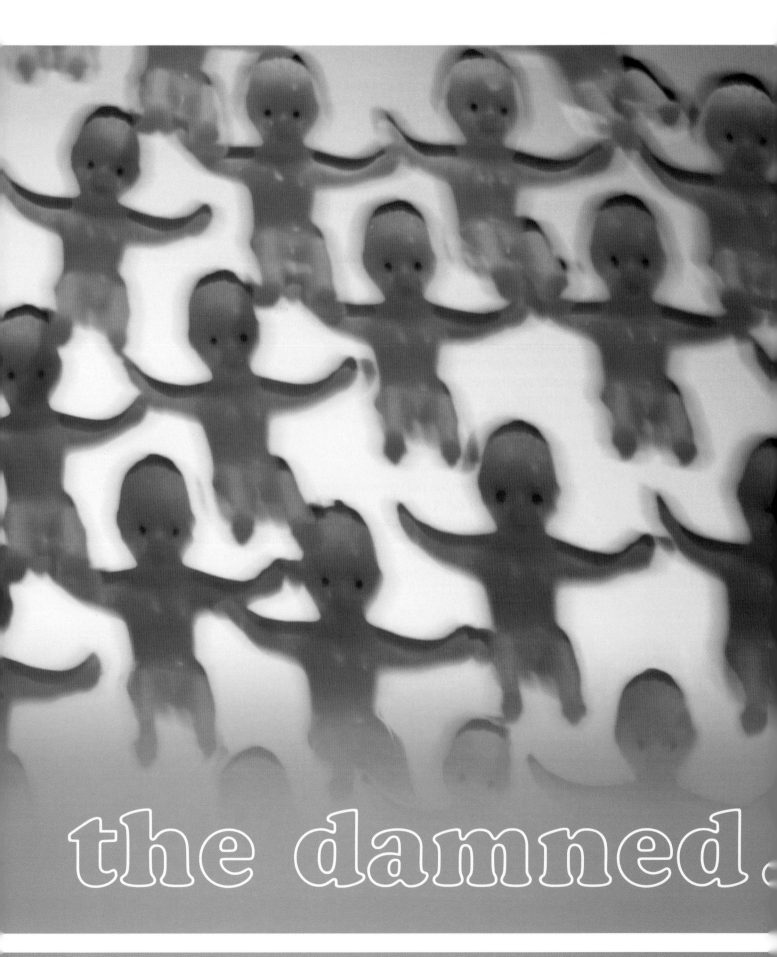

the damned.

The story opens with an extraordinary event which occurred on 26 September in the small village of Midwich. The narrator and his wife had been away from Midwich on that night and, on returning the following morning, found that the police would not let them enter the village. It appeared that there was some sort of invisible shield around the village and everyone inside the shield was unconscious. A few hours later, the whole village returned to normal and it was as if nothing had happened. The result of this strange occurrence, however, was apparent nine months later when nearly every woman in the village gave birth to a baby. It was generally agreed that these women were not the 'real mothers' but rather 'host mothers' to these babies which were human in form but had strange, golden eyes and unusual powers and were a result of what the villagers now called the 'Dayout'.

On the occasion she was referring to, Mrs Brant had gone into Mrs Welt's shop one morning to find her engaged in jabbing a pin into herself again and again, and weeping as she did it. This had not seemed good to Mrs Brant, so she had dragged her off to see Willers. He gave Mrs Welt some kind of sedative, and when she felt better she had explained that in changing the baby's napkin she had pricked him with a pin. Whereupon, by her account, the baby had just looked steadily at her with its golden eyes, and *made* her start jabbing the pin into herself.

As the Children grow, their powers increase and Zellaby, a man who lives in the village, relates a chilling event which he witnessed on one of his walks involving four of the Children.

Presently, the quartet in front rounded a corner and passed out of his sight. He had just reached the corner himself when a car overtook him, and he had, therefore, a clear view of all that followed.

The car, a small, open two-seater, was not travelling fast, but it happened that just round the corner, and shielded from sight by it, the Children had stopped. They appeared, still strung out across the road, to be debating which way they should go.

The car's driver did his best. He pulled hard over to the right in an attempt to avoid them, and all but succeeded. Another two inches, and he would have missed them entirely. But he could not make the extra inches. The tip of his left wing caught the outermost boy on the hip, and flung him across the road against the fence of a cottage garden.

There was a moment of tableau which remained quite static in Zellaby's mind. The boy against the fence, the three other Children frozen where they stood, the young man in the car in the act of straightening the wheels again, still braking.

Whether the car actually came to a stop Zellaby could never be sure; if it did it was for the barest instant, then the engine roared.

The car sprang forward. The driver changed up, and put his foot down again, keeping straight ahead. He made no attempt whatever to take the corner to the left. The car was still accelerating when it hit the churchyard wall. it smashed to smithereens, and hurled the driver headlong against the wall.

People shouted, and a few who were near started running towards the wreckage. Zellaby did not move. He stood half-stunned as he watched the yellow flames leap out, and the black smoke start upwards. Then, with a stiff-seeming movement, he turned to look at the Children. They, too, were staring at the wreck, a similar tense expression on each face. He had only a glimpse of it before it passed off, and the three of them turned to the boy who lay by the fence, groaning.

Zellaby became aware that he was trembling. He walked on a few yards, unsteadily, until he reached a seat by the edge of the Green. There he sat down and leant back, pale in the face, feeling ill.

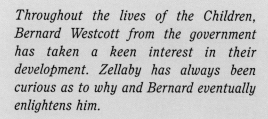

Throughout the lives of the Children, Bernard Westcott from the government has taken a keen interest in their development. Zellaby has always been curious as to why and Bernard eventually enlightens him.

'There's no longer any reason now, I think, why it should not have a restricted circulation,' Bernard admitted. 'I know that in the early stages you did quite a little inquiring into our own interest on your own account, Zellaby, but I don't believe you ever discovered the clue.'

'Which was?' inquired Zellaby.

'Simply that Midwich was not the only, nor even the first place to have a Dayout. Also, that during the three weeks around that time there was a marked rise in the radar detection of unidentified flying objects.'

'Well, I'm damned!' said Zellaby. 'Oh, vanity, vanity ...! There are *other* groups of Children beside ours, then? Where?'

But Bernard was not to be hurried, he continued deliberately:

'One Dayout took place at a small township in the Northern Territory of Australia. Something apparently went badly wrong there. There were thirty-three pregnancies, but for some reason the Children all died; most of them a few hours after birth, the eldest at a week old.

'There was another Dayout at an Eskimo settlement on Victoria Island, north of Canada. The inhabitants are cagey about what happened there, but it is believed that they were so outraged, or perhaps alarmed, at the arrival of babies so unlike their own kind that they exposed them almost at once. At any rate, none survived. And that, by the way, taken in conjunction with the time of the Midwich babies' return here, suggests that the power of duress does not develop until they are a week or two old, and that they may be truly individuals until then. Still another Dayout –'

Zellaby held up his hand.

'Let me guess. There was one behind the Iron Curtain.'

'There were two *known* ones behind the Curtain,' Bernard corrected him. One of them was in the Irkutsk region, near the border of Outer Mongolia – a very grim affair. It was assumed that the women had been lying with devils, and they perished, as well as the Children. The other was right away to the east, a place called Gizhinsk, in the mountains north-east of Okhotsk. There may have been others that we didn't hear of. It's pretty certain it happened in some places in South America and in Africa, too, but it's difficult to check. The inhabitants tend to be secretive. It's even possible that an isolated village would miss a day and not know it – in which case the babies would be even more of a puzzle. In most of the instances we do know of, the babies were regarded as freaks, and were killed, but we suspect that in some they may have been hidden away.'

'But not, I take it, in Gizhinsk?' put in Zellaby.

... 'The Far-East Army,' he said slowly, 'has recently been equipped with a new medium-type atomic cannon, believed to have a range of between fifty and sixty miles. Last week they carried out the first live tests with it. The town of Gizhinsk no longer exists ...

John Wyndham

TEXT LEVEL WORK

Comprehension

A 1 What reason did Mrs Brant give for jabbing herself with a pin?

2 After the driver had accidentally '*caught the outermost boy on the hip*', what did he do next?

3 How did Zellaby react to what he saw?

4 What startling news does Bernard give Zellaby about the 'Dayout'?

5 What happened in Gizhinsk?

B 1 Who do you think Willers is?

2 Explain the following in your own words:

a '*... all but succeeded ...*'
b '*... a restricted circulation ...*'
c '*... the Iron Curtain ...*'.

3 Why do you think the driver of the car '*made no attempt to take the corner to the left*'?

4 Explain in your own words why it was '*difficult to check*' if a 'Dayout' had occurred in South America and Africa.

C From the extracts, explain the impression that you have of:

• the Children
• Zellaby.

WORD LEVEL WORK

Vocabulary

Dictionary and contextual work
Use a dictionary and the context of the extract to explain the meaning of the following words:

1	quartet	7	apparently
2	debating	8	cagey
3	entirely	9	conjunction
4	tableau	10	duress
5	static	11	isolated
6	restricted	12	freaks

Spelling

Words ending in 'ary'
Key word: extraordin**ary**

1 Use this key word in a sentence of your own.

2 Learn these important 'ary' words:

imagin**ary**   necess**ary**
second**ary**   vocabul**ary**

SENTENCE LEVEL WORK

Grammar and punctuation

Direct speech

Remember the first four rules for punctuating direct speech:

1 Inverted commas are put before and after the spoken words.

2 Always use a capital letter when someone starts to speak.

3 Any words not actually spoken remain outside the inverted commas.

4 The punctuation of the words spoken comes inside the inverted commas.

Other rules or conventions for the punctuation of direct speech are:

5 Start a new paragraph every time the speaker changes, eg

'Which was?' inquired Zellaby.
'Simply that Midwich was not the only one,' said Bernard.

6 When words spoken form a sentence on their own, but are followed by a comma (not a full stop), the verb of saying and its subject come afterwards, eg

'There was one behind the Iron Curtain,' **Bernard said**.

7 When the subject and verb of saying start the sentence, use a comma before the inverted commas, to separate what is being said from the person saying it (the first word spoken has a capital letter), eg

Bernard continued deliberately, '**O**ne Dayout took place in Australia.'

8 If the spoken word is interrupted, or is two separate sentences spoken by the same person, inverted commas are used to show where speech begins and ends, eg

'There were two in Russia,' Bernard corrected him. 'One was in Mongolia – a very grim affair.'

9 When the 'spoken sentence' is broken, one comma is needed when breaking off the speech and another immediately before continuing it. The next word inside the inverted commas has a small letter, because it is a continuation of the spoken words, eg

'I know you did quite a lot of investigating, Zellaby,' Bernard admitted, '**b**ut I don't believe you ever discovered the clue.'

Copy these sentences. Put in the correct punctuation, layout and capitals.

1 the army he said slowly has recently been equipped with a new atomic cannon

2 but not I take it in gizhinsk put in zellaby

3 there was a marked rise in the radar detection of ufos bernard confirmed

4 well I'm damned said zellaby there are other groups of children beside ours

5 zellaby held up his hand exclaiming let me guess there was one in russia

6 last week they carried out the first live test said Bernard grimly the town of gizhinsk no longer exists

TEXT LEVEL WORK

Writing

First person narrative

> *The Midwich Cuckoos* is narrated in the first person.
>
> The narrator's role is not as a major character in the action but as an observer and recorder of the events.
>
> He was not in the village when the 'Dayout' occurred, but pieces together what had happened. He tells us:
>
> '*I have looked into the matter extensively*'.
>
> After having left the village for a few years he is drawn back in to what is happening there despite the fact that '*he had expected to hear that the whole thing had fizzled out.*' He couldn't have been more wrong!

Language features

Style and tone

The extraordinary events in Midwich are narrated in an almost matter-of-fact style. The narrator is like a policeman, recording the facts of the case without making any personal comments. The reader does not get the impression that the narrator is frightened or excited as he concentrates on describing the events.

Precise detail

Although the narrator was not present at much of what he is relating, he has investigated the various events and gives the reader precise details. He doesn't just record 'A car hit one of the Children', he gives details of:

- its type and size: '*The car, a small, open two seater ...*'
- its speed: '*... was not travelling fast ...*'
- how close it came to missing the Children: '*Another two inches...*'.

He is able to record not only what Zellaby looked liked after he witnessed the crash – '*pale in the face*' – but it is obvious he has spoken to Zellaby because he can tell the readers that he '*became aware that he was trembling and he was feeling ill*'.

Writing assignment

Take on the role of the narrator and relate another strange incident which could have occurred in Midwich where the Children demonstrate their chilling power. You can either:

- have witnessed the incident yourself on a visit to Midwich
  or
- relate the event as it was told to you.

Write in the same matter-of-fact style and use precise detail.

Personal choice

Choose one of the following assignments.

1 Continue the conversation between Zellaby and Bernard to make it clear how both react to what has happened to the Children in various places.

2 Write a diary entry as Mrs Welt for the day she was '*made to start jabbing the pin into herself*'. How does she feel towards the baby? How does she feel about the future?

Have reason to suspect attic

Fahrenheit 451 is Ray Bradbury's hauntingly prophetic novel of a weird but not too distant future where happiness is allocated on a four-walled TV screen, where individuals, eccentrics and scholars are outcasts of society and where books – the cause of all unhappiness and disruption – are burned by a special task-force of firemen.

It is also the story of Montag, trained by the state to be a destroyer, who one day throws down his can of kerosene and begins to read a book.

FAHRENHEIT 451: the temperature at which book-paper catches fire and burns

It was a flaking three-storey house in the ancient part of the city, a century old if it was a day, but like all houses it had been given a thin fireproof plastic sheath many years ago, and this preservative shell seemed to be the only thing holding it in the sky.

'Here we are!'

The engine slammed to a stop, Beatty, Stoneman, and Black ran up the sidewalk, suddenly odious and fat in the plump fireproof slickers. Montag followed.

They crashed the front door and grabbed at a woman, though she was not running, she was not trying to escape. She was only standing, weaving from side to side, her eyes fixed upon a nothingness in the wall as if they had struck her a terrible blow upon the head. Her tongue was moving in her mouth, and her eyes seemed to be trying to remember something, and then they remembered and her tongue moved again:

'"Play the man, Master Ridley; we shall this day light such a candle, by God's grace, in England, as I trust shall never be put out."'

'Enough of that!' said Beatty. 'Where are they?'

He slapped her face with amazing objectivity and repeated the question. The old woman's eyes came to a focus upon Beatty. 'You know where they are or you wouldn't be here,' she said.

Stoneman held out the telephone alarm card with the complaint signed in telephone duplicate on the back:

'Have reason to suspect attic; 11 No. Elm, City.
                                                E. B.'

'That would be Mrs Blake, my neighbour,' said the woman, reading the initials.

'All right, men, let's get 'em!'

Next thing they were up in the musty blackness, swinging silver hatches at doors that were, after all, unlocked, tumbling through like boys all rollick and shout. 'Hey!' A fountain of books sprang down upon Montag as he climbed shuddering up the sheer stairwell. How inconvenient! Always before it had been like snuffing a candle. The police went first and adhesive-taped the victim's mouth and bandaged him off into their glittering beetle cars, so when you arrived you found an empty house. You weren't hurting anyone, you were hurting only *things*! And since things really couldn't be hurt, since things felt nothing, and things don't scream or whimper, as this woman might begin to scream and cry out, there was nothing to tease your conscience later. You were simply cleaning up. Janitorial work, essentially. Everything to its proper place. Quick with the kerosene! Who's got a match!

But now, tonight, someone had slipped. This woman was spoiling the ritual. The men were making too much noise, laughing, joking to cover her terrible accusing silence below. She made the empty rooms roar with accusation and shake down a fine dust of guilt that was sucked in their nostrils as they plunged about. It was neither cricket nor correct. Montag felt an immense irritation. She shouldn't be here, on top of everything!

Books bombarded his shoulders, his arms, his upturned face. A book alighted, almost obediently, like a white pigeon, in his hands, wings fluttering. In the dim, wavering light, a page hung open and it was like a snowy feather, the words delicately painted thereon. In all the rush and fervour, Montag had only an instant to read a line, but it blazed in his mind for the next minute as if stamped there with fiery steel. 'Time has fallen asleep in the afternoon sunshine.' He dropped the book. Immediately, another fell into his arms.

'Montag, up here!'

Montag's hand closed like a mouth, crushed the book with wild devotion, with an insanity of mindlessness to his chest. The men above were hurling shovelfuls of magazines into the dusty air. They fell like slaughtered birds and the woman stood below, like a small girl, among the bodies.

Montag had done nothing. His hand had done it all, his hand, with a brain of its own, with a conscience and curiosity in each trembling finger, had turned thief. Now, it plunged the book back under his arm, pressed it right to the sweating armpit, rushed out empty, with a magician's flourish! Look here! Innocent! Look!

He gazed, shaken, at that white hand. He held it way out, as if he were far-sighted. He held it close, as if he were blind.

'Montag!'

He jerked about.

'Don't stand there, idiot!'

The books lay like great mounds of fishes left to dry. The men danced and slipped and fell over them. Titles glittered their golden eyes, falling, gone.

'Kerosene!'

They pumped the cold fluid from the numbered 451 tanks strapped to their shoulders. They coated each book, they pumped rooms full of it.

They hurried downstairs, Montag staggered after them in the kerosene fumes.

'Come on, woman!'

The woman knelt among the books, touching the drenched leather and cardboard, reading the gilt titles with her fingers while her eyes accused Montag.

'You can't ever have my books,' she said.

'You know the law,' said Beatty. 'Where's your common sense? None of those books agree with each other. You've been locked up here for years with a regular damned Tower of Babel. Snap out of it! The people in those books never lived. Come on now!'

She shook her head.

'The whole house is going up,' said Beatty.

The men walked clumsily to the door. They glanced back at Montag, who stood near the woman.

'You're not leaving her here?' he protested.

'She won't come.'

'Force her, then!'

Beatty raised his hand in which was concealed the igniter. 'We're due back at the house. Beside, these fanatics always try suicide; the pattern's familiar.'

Montag placed his hands on the woman's elbow. 'You can come with me.'

'No,' she said. 'Thank you, anyway.'

'I'm counting to ten,' said Beatty. 'One. Two.'

'Please,' said Montag.

'Go on,' said the woman.

'Three. Four.'

'Here.' Montag pulled at the woman.

The woman replied quietly, 'I want to stay here.'

'Five. Six.'

'You can stop counting,' she said. She opened the fingers of one hand slightly and in the palm of the hand was a single slender object.

An ordinary kitchen match.

Ray Bradbury

TEXT LEVEL WORK

Comprehension

A 1 What is the significance of the temperature '*Farenheit 451*'?

2 How did the 'firemen' know that there were books at the woman's house?

3 Who usually went in before the firemen?

4 What did Montag do with:

   a the first book which fell into his hands

   b the second book which fell into his hands?

   5 What did the men use to ensure the books burnt easily?

B 1 What is the first clue the reader gets that Montag is not 'one of the gang'?

   2 How does Montag justify to himself what he does for a living?

   3 What impression do the phrases '*fell like slaughtered birds*' and '*lay like great mounds of fishes left to dry*' give the reader of the destruction of the books?

   4 Why do you think the woman having a match could be dangerous to them all?

C Quoting evidence from the extract to support your answer, explain the impressions you get of the following characters:

   • Montag   • Beatty   • the woman.

WORD LEVEL WORK

Vocabulary

Dictionary and contextual work

Use a dictionary and the context of the extract to explain the meaning of the following words:

1 prophetic	4 objectivity	7 janitorial	10 protested
2 eccentrics	5 musty	8 ritual	11 concealed
3 odious	6 inconvenient	9 fervour	12 fanatics

Spelling

Double 'l' words

Key words: allocated   rollick   really   essentially

   1 Use these key words in sentences of your own.

   2 Learn these important double 'l' words:

   parallel   collage   collection   Illusion   gallery

SENTENCE LEVEL WORK

Grammar and punctuation

Reported speech

> When you want to use your own writing voice to report what somebody else said, you don't need quotation marks. The following rules govern the punctuation and structure changes of reported speech.
>
> • For all reported speech:
>   – remove quotation marks and internal capital letters
>   – change pronouns.
> • Reporting statements:
>   – add the word 'that'
>   – shift verbs one step back in time, eg
>
>   The young woman whispered, 'I think I love him.'
>   *becomes*
>   The young woman whispered **that** she **thought** she loved him.

- Reporting commands, invitations, requests:
  - shift verbs to infinitives, adjusting reporting words to fit, eg

    The teacher said, 'Be quiet, Michael. Show some respect for fellow students.'

    becomes

    The teacher told Michael **to be quiet** and **to respect** his fellow students.

- Reporting yes/no questions:
  - remove both quotation marks and question mark
  - add 'whether' or 'if'
  - take verbs out of question order and shift them one step back in time, eg

    The pupil asked, 'Is this a quotation?'

    becomes

    The pupil asked **if** that **was** a quotation.

- Reporting information questions:
  - remove both quotation marks and question mark
  - keep the question word
  - take verbs out of question order and shift them one step back in time, eg

    His wife asked, 'Why do you think it's a fraud?'

    becomes

    His wife asked **why** he **thought** it **was** a fraud.

Copy each of the following direct speech sentences and, underneath them, write the reported speech version of each sentence.

1 'Enough of that!' said Beatty.

2 'That would be Mrs Blake, my neighbour,' said the woman, reading the initials.

3 'You know the law,' said Beatty.

4 Montag protested, 'You're not leaving her here?'

5 The woman replied quietly, 'I want to stay here.'

6 'No,' she said. 'Thank you, anyway.'

TEXT LEVEL WORK

Writing

Characterisation

The extract from *Fahrenheit 451* is a turning point in the story as we see Montag, trained by the state to be a destroyer, changing and developing as a character. He turns away from burning books to wanting to read them, an action which causes him to question his way of life and those who rule the state in which he lives.

Language features

Characterisation

Being able to create believable characters is one of the signs of good quality writing. When those characters are human beings they should not simply be 'good' or 'bad'. Montag is a 'state destroyer' and, up to this point in the story, has never questioned what he does but we see how his attitude is changing:

- he does not batter down the front door and grab the woman as the others do
- in the middle of all the destruction, he takes and hides a book
- he is concerned that the woman does not burn with her house unlike the others who are happy to leave her.

The defining moment

In the extract we sense that Montag is not totally convinced by what he is doing. His workmates are 'suddenly odious' and he is irritated that the woman is there and has not been taken away by the police. If he does not see the people whose lives he is wrecking, he can cope and justify what he is doing as he has so many times before. This is different. It is Montag's defining moment when his life changes forever because of that book which 'fell into his arms'.

Dialogue and actions

A good way to let your reader see what type of person a character is, is through dialogue and action, eg

	Dialogue	Action
Beatty	'these fanatics always try suicide'	'He slapped her face with amazing objectivity'
Montag	'You're not leaving her here?	'Montag pulled at the woman.'

Vocabulary choices

The writer conveys the brutality and the joy of destruction in the extract through careful vocabulary choices. The impression given is one of violent and frenzied activity, through the choice of vocabulary such as: 'slammed', 'crashed', 'grabbed', 'slapped', 'swinging', 'tumbling', 'hurling shovelfuls', 'danced and slipped and fell over them'.

Writing assignment

Write about a character whose attitude to what he or she does changes throughout the narrative. You should:

- decide what job your character does or what situation he/she finds themselves in
- make it clear that up to this point the character has not thought too deeply about the effects of what he/she does and just goes along with the others
- describe the defining moment when your character undergoes a change of heart and is now obviously different in his/her attitude to the others.

Personal choice

Choose one of the following assignments.

1 Imagine you are the woman in the house. You know that your neighbour has informed against you to the firemen and that they will be here in the next ten minutes. Write your thoughts and feelings.

2 Imagine Montag has been seen hiding the book by one of the other firemen. As Montag, what could you say to persuade the man that reading books is right and destroying books is wrong. Write your conversation.

Published in 2003 by:
Nelson Thornes Ltd
Delta Place
27 Bath Road
CHELTENHAM
GL53 7TH
United Kingdom

03 04 05 06 07 / 10 9 8 7 6 5 4 3 2 1

A catalogue record for this book is available from the British Library

ISBN 0-7487-6947-1

Illustrations by Martin Berry and Paul Gardiner
Designed by Viners Wood Associates

Printed and bound in Spain by Graficas Estella

Acknowledgements
The authors and publishers are grateful to the following for permission to reproduce photographs and other copyright material in this book:

Cambridge University Press for material from Bill Forsyth, *Gregory's Girl*, Act Now Series (1983) pp. 14-18; Don Congdon Associates, Inc on behalf of the author for material from Ray Bradbury, *Fahrenheit 451*, pp. 40-44. Copyright © 1953, renewed 1981 by Ray Bradbury; Curtis Brown Ltd, New York on behalf of the Estate of the author for Ogden Nash, 'Confessions of a Born Spectator', first published in *The New Yorker* (1937). Copyright © 1937 by Ogden Nash, renewed; Faber and Faber Ltd for T S Eliot, 'The Journey of the Magi' from *Collected Poems 1909-1962* by T S Eliot; A M Heath & Co Ltd on behalf of Bill Hamilton as the Literary Executor of the Estate of the late Sonia Brownell Orwell and Secker and Warburg Ltd for material from George Orwell, *Animal Farm* (1945), pp. 16-7, 76-8. Copyright © George Orwell 1945; David Higham Associates on behalf of the author for material from John Wyndham, *The Midwich Cuckoos*, Michael Joseph (1957) pp. 138-9, 188-90, 191; Bobbi Katz for 'Skiing'. Copyright © 1971 by Bobbi Katz; Peter Newbolt for Henry Newbolt, 'Vitai Lampada' from *Selected Poems of Henry Newbolt*, Hodder & Stoughton (1981). Copyright © Peter Newbolt; Penguin Books Ltd for material from Apollonius of Rhodes,*The Voyage of Argo (The Argonautica)*, trans. by E V Rieu, Penguin Classics, 1950, pp. 82, 88-90. Copyright © the Estate of E V Rieu, 1959; and Barry Hines, *A Kestrel for a Knave*, Michael Joseph (1968) pp. 86-9. Copyright © Barry Hines, 1968; The Random House Group Ltd for material from Anthony Burgess, *A Clockwork Orange*, Willian Heinemann (1962) pp. 6-8; Rogers Coleridge & White Ltd on behalf of the author for material from Marjorie Darke, *The First of Midnight*, Kestrel Books (1977). Copyright © Marjorie Darke 1977; Paul Simon Music for Paul Simon, 'Homeward Bound'. Copyright © 1966 Paul Simon; Sony/ATV Music Publishing for Bob Dylan, 'With God On Our Side'; Warner Bos for material from 'Rebel Without A Cause'.

Corbis, p.16, 34, 100; Corel 510 (NT), p.82; Peter Adams/Digital Vision BP (NT), p.22; Joe Cornish/Digital Vision LL (NT) p.28; Getty images, p.29, 64; Photodisk 41 (NT), p.106; Roland Grant Archive, p.4, 52, 58, 70, 76, 88; Courtesy of S4C International, p.46; Shakespeare Birthplace Trust, p.40

Every effort has been made to trace the copyright holders but if any have been inadvertently overlooked the publishers will be pleased to make the necessary arrangement at the first opportunity.